Renewable Energy Projects Don't Fail on Technology — They Fail on Execution

OrangeBooks Publication

1st Floor, Rajhans Arcade, Mall Road, Kohka, Bhilai, Chhattisgarh 490020

Website: **www.orangebooks.in**

First Edition, 2026

ISBN: 978-93-7426-843-8

Price: Rs. 375.00

Printed in India

RENEWABLE ENERGY PROJECTS

DON'T FAIL ON TECHNOLOGY – THEY FAIL ON EXECUTION

Technology is Ready, Execution is the Challenge

Success is built on Execution, Not just Technology

Turning Plans into Reality - On Time and On Ground

DR. VIPUL JAMBUCHA

OrangeBooks Publication
www.orangebooks.in

Dedicated to

My Mother

Late. Mrs. Manjulaben Babubhai Jambucha

My first teacher, my greatest strength, and my silent inspiration.

You left this world too soon, but your values continue to guide every step I take.

This book exists because you existed in my life.

Your blessings remain with me. Always.

Author Profile

— Dr. Vipul Jambucha

Dr. Vipul Jambucha is a renewable energy leader and project management professional, with long **experience in project management** and specially in **the renewable energy sector**, spanning wind, solar, and emerging green energy projects across India and abroad.

Dr. Vipul Jambucha has led and delivered large-scale renewable energy projects in complex, high-pressure environments involving land acquisition, grid evacuation, EPC execution, regulatory coordination, and stakeholder management. His work sits at the intersection of **strategy and site reality**, where ambitious plans are tested by execution discipline.

Over his career, Dr. Vipul Jambucha has worked with leading national and international organizations, contributing to projects that demanded precision, accountability, and on-the-ground leadership rather than theoretical planning.

With his vast experience in the renewable energy project sector, Dr. Vipul Jambucha is known for advocating an **execution-first culture**, where ownership, governance, and delivery reliability matter more than presentations, targets, or technology claims.

Through his writing and leadership, he champions the belief that **India's energy transition will be won not by ambition alone, but by leaders who can consistently convert intent into commissioned assets—on time and on ground**.

This book reflects his lived experience of building, fixing, and delivering renewable energy projects where execution—not technology—determined success.

Author's Note

This book is written from the ground—where solar modules meet soil, wind turbines meet terrain, and plans meet reality. After decades in project management and renewable energy leadership, one truth stands clear: technology rarely causes failure; execution almost always does.

Please share your comment or review on author's email id: jambuchavb@gmail.com or you can send a message on his linkedin profile @Dr.Vipul Jamhucha

Linkedin Link: https://www.linkedin.com/in/dr-vipul-jambucha-phd-pmp-b2410881/

Book Synopsis

Overview

Despite unprecedented momentum, capital inflow, and technological maturity, renewable energy projects across India and other emerging markets continue to suffer from delays, cost overruns, stranded assets, and eroding investor confidence. The common explanation—technology limitations or policy uncertainty—has become a convenient but misleading narrative.

This book challenges that narrative

"Why Renewable Energy Projects Don't Fail on Technology — They Fail on Execution" is a leadership and execution handbook written from the ground up, by a renewable energy CEO and project professional who has spent decades navigating land, grid, governance, people, and commercial realities across solar and wind projects.

The book's central argument is clear and uncompromising

Technology enables renewable projects. Execution determines whether they succeed or fail.

What the Book Explores

The book systematically dismantles the most common myths surrounding renewable project failure and replaces them with execution-first truths:

- Why world-class technology still produces delayed and underperforming projects
- How projects silently fail between approval and commissioning

- Why land and evacuation are not technical issues, but leadership challenges
- How governance collapses into firefighting under pressure
- Why coordination failures quietly destroy margins
- How people, not processes, decide outcomes
- Why false urgency and WhatsApp-driven management erode execution quality
- How ignored risks and weak ownership mature into crises
- Why EPC–developer mistrust slows delivery despite strong contracts
- How policy is often blamed for failures rooted in unpreparedness
- Why time is the most expensive and irreversible project resource

Each chapter is supported by **India-specific execution case boxes**, drawn from real project patterns, making the book deeply practical and immediately relatable.

Index

Chapter - 1

The Great Technology Myth

Technology Was Never the Problem

If technology were the real reason renewable energy projects failed, this industry would have collapsed long ago.

Solar modules today are more efficient than what powered utility-scale plants just a decade ago. Wind turbines have crossed capacity factors that were once considered impossible. SCADA systems provide real-time visibility.

Financing structures are mature. Policies, though imperfect, are largely supportive.

And yet—projects still Miss CODs. Costs escalate quietly. Assets sit idle, waiting for evacuation. Teams burn out. Investors grow cautious.

As a lifelong project professional, I have reviewed enough delayed projects to say this without hesitation:

Technology rarely fails. Execution does.

This is not a popular statement. It is far more comfortable to blame module quality, turbine availability, or changing specifications. Technology is an easy scapegoat—it doesn't argue back. Execution, on the other hand, forces uncomfortable questions about planning, ownership, and leadership.

The Comfort of the Technology Narrative

The renewable energy sector loves technology narratives. Conferences showcase the next-generation module. Pitch decks highlight turbine ratings. LinkedIn posts celebrate innovation.

Technology feels progressive. Execution feels mundane.

But here is the uncomfortable truth: no project has ever failed because technology was 1% less efficient than promised. Projects fail because land wasn't ready, approvals weren't aligned, grid timelines were assumed, or risks were ignored.

I have seen projects with world-class equipment fail to commission on time. I have also seen average technology deliver exceptional returns—because execution was disciplined.

Technology is visible. Execution is invisible until it breaks.

Execution is Not a Soft Skill

One of the most damaging myths in renewable energy is that execution is a "management issue" rather than a technical discipline.

Execution is engineering with consequences.

It requires sequencing. Dependencies. Risk buffers. Governance. Decision velocity. Accountability.

A project does not move forward because someone works harder. It moves forward because the right decision is taken at the right time by the right owner.

Execution excellence is not built in boardrooms. It is built in how land teams talk to engineering, how finance aligns with procurement, how EPC mobilization follows—not precedes—readiness.

Where Projects Actually Break

Projects do not collapse dramatically. They erode.

A missed land parcel here. A delayed approval there. An evacuation assumption that quietly slips by two months. A payment cycle that strains contractors.

Individually, these look manageable. Collectively, they become fatal.

Execution failure is rarely one big mistake. It is the accumulation of small ignored risks.

And the most dangerous phrase in any renewable project is:

"We will manage it later."

Later always arrives—with interest.

My Uncomfortable Realization

When I first transitioned into senior leadership, I believed strategy and vision were the hardest parts of my role.

I was wrong.

The hardest part is insisting on execution discipline when optimism is high and pressure is mounting.

It is far easier to announce capacity targets than to ask whether land is genuinely secured. Easier to sign EPC contracts than to verify readiness. Easier to demand speed than to invest in planning.

Leadership failure in renewables is rarely about intent. It is about tolerance for weak execution.

Technology Enables. Execution Decides

Technology opens the door. Execution determines whether you walk through it—or trip at the threshold.

In the chapters that follow, we will dismantle the illusion that better machines guarantee success. We will examine land, evacuation, governance, people, risk, and time—the real forces that shape outcomes.

If there is one idea to carry forward from this chapter, let it be this:

The renewable energy transition will not be won by those with the best technology, but by those who can execute reliably, repeatedly, and responsibly.

Because in this industry, ambition is common.

Execution excellence is rare.

The Silent Cost of Poor Execution

The real damage of execution failure is not only measured in delayed CODs or liquidated damages.

It is measured in credibility.

In India's renewable ecosystem, credibility travels faster than any official performance report. Developers, lenders, EPC contractors, land aggregators and utilities remember who consistently delivers—and who always needs "one more extension."

Every delayed project quietly raises three uncomfortable questions in the market

- Can this team be trusted with larger capacity?
- Can this promoter absorb operational complexity?
- Can this organization scale without collapsing under its own processes?

Technology cannot repair a damaged reputation.

Only execution can.

Ironically, many renewable companies invest more time selecting inverter brands than selecting project leaders.

We obsess over equipment warranties but treat delivery ownership as an afterthought.

In a capital-intensive industry, execution credibility becomes financial capital.

Banks may never say it openly, but they price execution maturity into every appraisal.

So do investors.

So do serious EPC partners.

Execution is not only operational discipline.

It is financial discipline.

Why Smart Teams Still Execute Poorly

One of the most confusing realities I have observed is this

Execution failures rarely come from incompetent people.

They come from well-qualified professionals working inside poorly designed systems.

Most renewable organizations grow faster than their execution architecture. They expand portfolios, geographies and technology stacks—but continue to run projects using informal coordination, spreadsheet-based tracking and hero-driven firefighting.

The organization looks strong on paper.

But underneath, it is fragile.

Typical symptoms appear early

Land acquisition and engineering run on parallel assumptions rather than synchronized milestones.

Evacuation timelines are discussed, not contractually locked.

Procurement is driven by commercial opportunity rather than site readiness.

Construction planning assumes approvals will arrive "as usual."

Finance releases mobilization advances without enforceable readiness gates.

Everyone is busy.

Very few are aligned.

Execution collapses not because people do not care—but because no single system forces reality to surface early.

The Illusion of Speed

In today's renewable market, speed is celebrated aggressively.

Fast closures.

Fast financial sanctions.

Fast EPC awards.

Fast site mobilization.

Speed makes for great headlines and investor decks.

But in real project delivery, speed without readiness is not acceleration—it is risk compression.

By compressing decision cycles without compressing uncertainty, projects only move problems forward in time. They do not remove them.

The pressure to "start work" often becomes more powerful than the responsibility to confirm whether work should start at all.

True execution maturity shows up when leadership is willing to slow down at the right moments.

Not to delay projects—but to prevent delayed projects.

A one-week delay in contract finalization can save a six-month delay in commissioning.

But this trade-off rarely survives leadership impatience.

Readiness is Not a Checklist

Most organizations treat project readiness as a static checklist.

Land: yes/no

Evacuation: yes/no

Approvals: in progress

EPC: appointed

Finance: arranged

This binary thinking is dangerously simplistic.

Readiness is dynamic.

It has depth, quality and reliability.

Land is not ready because papers are signed.

It is ready when access roads exist, boundaries are undisputed, local resistance is managed and site possession is legally and socially defensible.

Evacuation is not ready because a substation is planned.

It is ready when transmission schedules, shutdown windows, utility interfaces and statutory approvals are locked into a realistic construction sequence.

Permits are not ready because applications are filed.

They are ready when dependencies are understood and timelines are contractually defensible.

Execution leadership demands a far more nuanced understanding of readiness than dashboards typically show.

The Real Role of Leadership in Execution

Leadership does not execute projects.

Organizations do.

But leadership defines what execution quality is allowed to look like.

The most damaging leadership behavior I see in renewable projects is silent tolerance.

Tolerance for weak planning.

Tolerance for unclear ownership.

Tolerance for unrealistic schedules.

Tolerance for optimistic reporting.

When senior leaders accept partial truth to preserve momentum, execution culture decays quietly.

The first casualty is transparency.

The second is accountability.

The third is trust.

Great execution cultures are not aggressive.

They are brutally clear.

They demand

- Named owners for every critical dependency
- Time-bound decisions, not endless discussions
- Formal escalation paths before issues become crises

- Clear authority to stop mobilization when readiness collapses

In such environments, bad news travels upward early.

In weak environments, bad news travels downward until it explodes.

Governance is Execution Infrastructure

Most renewable organizations invest heavily in technology platforms but underinvest in execution governance.

Governance is not about committees.

It is about decision structure.

Who can approve scope changes?

Who can freeze design?

Who can re-sequence construction?

Who owns interface risks between EPC, transmission and land teams?

When governance is unclear, decisions slow down.

When decisions slow down, teams improvise.

When teams improvise, risk multiplies.

Execution excellence depends on predictable decision velocity.

Not fast decisions.

Consistent decisions.

A project does not fail because one decision was wrong.

It fails because dozens of decisions were delayed, diluted or delegated without authority.

People are the Hardest Technology

In renewable projects, we treat equipment as critical assets.

We rarely treat execution leaders the same way.

Yet project leadership is the single most irreplaceable asset in delivery.

A strong project head absorbs uncertainty without passing chaos to the field.

A weak project head transmits every ambiguity directly to contractors.

Execution is emotional work.

It requires

- Conflict management between stakeholders
- Negotiation under time pressure
- Escalation without politics
- Resilience when plans collapse

No digital tool can substitute for mature leadership behavior under stress.

Organizations that rotate project leaders too frequently, overload high performers or treat delivery roles as stepping stones rather than professional disciplines slowly destroy execution capability from within.

Risk Registers That Nobody Uses

Almost every renewable project maintains a risk register. Very few actually manage risk.

The register becomes a document created for lenders, auditors or internal reviews—not a live execution tool.

True risk management is uncomfortable. It forces teams to acknowledge

- Uncertain land closures
- Fragile utility commitments
- Local political sensitivities
- Contractor cash flow fragility
- Internal capability gaps

Most execution failures occur because known risks are accepted without credible mitigation.

Hope becomes the mitigation strategy. Hope is not a project control mechanism.

India-Specific Reality: Institutional Interfaces

In the Indian context, execution complexity increases dramatically at institutional boundaries.

Projects do not fail inside EPC sites.

They fail at interfaces

- Between developers and utilities
- Between state agencies and contractors
- Between land aggregators and local communities
- Between lenders and promoters

These interfaces are not technical.

They are institutional and human.

No turbine specification can resolve unclear utility coordination.

No module efficiency can accelerate statutory approvals.

Execution leadership in India must be exceptionally strong in relationship governance—not only contract management.

This capability is rarely taught.

It is learned painfully, project after project.

The Execution Debt We Create

Every shortcut taken in early development creates execution debt.

Every informal assurance creates execution debt.

Every conditional approval creates execution debt.

Every provisional land handover creates execution debt.

Like financial debt, execution debt compounds.

It appears manageable at small scale.

It becomes catastrophic at portfolio scale.

Organizations that grow aggressively without reducing execution debt eventually reach a point where no new project can be delivered without fixing old problems first.

That moment is usually called a “temporary slowdown.”

In reality, it is an execution reckoning.

The Discipline Nobody Celebrates

Execution excellence is not glamorous

There are no awards for clean land handovers.

No social media posts for aligned evacuation schedules.

No stage applause for realistic commissioning plans.

But these invisible disciplines determine whether renewable growth is sustainable—or merely impressive on paper.

As leaders, our real responsibility is not to announce capacity.

It is to build delivery systems that can absorb complexity without breaking people, partners or credibility.

Closing Reflection

Technology will continue to improve.

Costs will continue to decline.

Innovation will continue to excite.

But renewable energy is no longer an experimental sector.

It is infrastructure. And infrastructure demands operational maturity far beyond enthusiasm.

The great technology myth distracts us from a far more difficult truth:

Most renewable failures are not engineering failures.

They are organizational failures.

Until leadership begins treating execution as a strategic capability—not a project function—the industry will continue repeating the same mistakes under newer technologies and larger capacities.

Progress in renewables will not be limited by innovation. It will be limited by our willingness to professionalize execution.

And that is not a technology problem. It is a leadership choice.

Chapter - 2

From Vision to Commissioning–Where Projects Actually Break

The Most Dangerous Space in a Renewable Project.

Every renewable energy project begins with confidence.

A vision is approved. A capacity number is announced.

A timeline is committed. Financial models look robust. Presentations are optimistic.

And then the project enters its most dangerous phase—the space between approval and commissioning.

This is where most renewable projects do not collapse, but quietly lose control.

Not because the vision was wrong. Not because the technology was unproven.

But because execution complexity was underestimated.

The Myth of Linear Progress

On paper, projects move in clean, linear stages

Approval → Land → Design → Procurement → Construction → Commissioning

In reality, execution is not linear. It is interdependent.

Land impacts layout. Layout impacts evacuation.

Evacuation impacts approvals. Approvals impact financing. Financing impacts procurement. Procurement impacts schedules.

When one element slips, everything else absorbs the shock.

A project does not move at the speed of its fastest function. It moves at the speed of its weakest dependency.

Where Projects Start Bleeding, projects rarely fail at a single dramatic moment. They bleed in phases.

Phase 1: Assumptions Replace Verification

Land is "mostly secured."

Evacuation is "expected on time."

Approvals are "in process."

Execution does not tolerate assumptions—it demands confirmation.

Phase 2: Parallel Work Without Readiness

To save time, teams begin working in parallel:

- EPC mobilizes before land handover
- Procurement advances before final drawings
- Contractors are pressured before payment clarity

Parallel execution without readiness does not accelerate projects—it amplifies risk.

Phase 3: Silence Replaces Escalation

Early warning signs are visible:

- Small land disputes
- Minor approval delays
- Vendor discomfort

But escalation is avoided in the name of optimism.

This silence is expensive.

The Commissioning Illusion

Commissioning is often treated as a technical milestone.

In truth, commissioning is the final audit of execution discipline.

By the time a project reaches commissioning

- All execution decisions have already been made
- All shortcuts have already been taken - All risks have already matured

Technology only reveals what execution has built.

The Execution Gap Nobody Owns

Between vision and commissioning lies a gap that rarely has a single owner.

Strategy teams move on.

Finance focuses on disbursements.

Engineering completes designs.

EPCs focus on scope.

Execution falls between functions.

Execution excellence demands an empowered project leader with authority across functions.

Without this, projects do not fail—they drift.

My Hard Lesson

Early in my leadership journey, I believed frequent reviews would prevent execution failure.

They did not.

Reviews report progress.

They do not create readiness.

What prevents failure is uncomfortable questioning

- Is land fully handed over—or assumed?
- Is evacuation scheduled—or promised?
- Is cash flow aligned with construction pace?

Execution discipline is not about more meetings.

It is about better questions.

From Vision to Commissioning—The Only Path That Works

Projects that move smoothly share common traits:

- Dependencies mapped before timelines
- Readiness gates before commitments
- Escalation encouraged, not punished
- Singular execution ownership

They do not avoid problems. They confront them early.

The Backbone of Execution

Vision inspires projects. Technology enables them.

But execution carries them.

If Chapter 1 dismantled the technology myth, this chapter exposes the execution gap.

The next chapters dive deeper—starting with the most underestimated risk of all: land.

Because renewable projects do not break at commissioning.

They break much earlier—when execution is assumed instead of designed.

The Space Nobody Designs For

In most renewable organizations, enormous effort is invested in shaping the beginning of the project and celebrating the end of the project.

Very little effort is invested in designing the middle.

The middle is where execution lives.

The transition from concept approval to physical site readiness is rarely treated as a formal project phase. It is treated as a "mobilisation period," a prelude to real work.

But this is precisely the phase where execution architecture should be built.

If this phase is weak, the project may still start.

It will almost certainly not finish cleanly.

The most dangerous space in a renewable project is not construction.

It is the undefined space between commitment and control.

When Commitments Outrun Capability

One pattern appears repeatedly in delayed renewable projects.

Commercial commitments are signed before operational capability is fully assessed.

Tariffs are locked.

Delivery dates are announced.

LD clauses are accepted.

Power sale agreements are concluded.

But the internal question—*can this organization realistically deliver this specific project, at this specific location, within this specific timeline, using its current people, partners and processes?*—is rarely answered honestly.

Organizations overestimate what systems can absorb and underestimate how quickly execution friction multiplies.

Capacity ambition expands faster than execution maturity.

This is how projects begin with confidence and end with excuses.

The Real Bottleneck is Not Construction

In post-project reviews, construction delays are usually blamed.

But construction is only the visible bottleneck.

The real bottleneck lies upstream

- Unclear land access
- Incomplete geotechnical understanding
- Evolving layouts
- Uncertain right-of-way routes
- Ambiguous utility interfaces
- Delayed statutory sequencing

Construction teams cannot move faster than clarity.

No site team can outperform an ambiguous project definition.

Execution breaks long before boots touch the ground.

Interdependencies are Not Risks — They are Design Inputs

In renewable projects, interdependencies are often treated as external risks.

In reality, they are internal design parameters.

Land closure is not a risk.

It is a schedule design input.

Evacuation readiness is not a risk.

It is a construction sequence design input.

Utility coordination is not a risk.

It is a commissioning design input.

When these interdependencies are treated as uncertain variables rather than fixed design drivers, schedules become speculative narratives rather than executable plans.

This is why many project plans look beautiful—and collapse on first contact with reality.

The Hidden Damage of Parallel Execution

Parallel execution is usually justified as a time-saving strategy.

But parallel execution without firm readiness is not project acceleration.

It is organizational stress testing.

Each parallel activity creates contractual, financial and operational exposure.

When EPC mobilisation begins before land readiness, the project creates idle cost.

When procurement is triggered before design freeze, the project creates rework.

When subcontractors are engaged before payment certainty, the project creates fragility in its supply chain.

Parallel execution is powerful only when uncertainty has already been reduced.

Otherwise, it simply distributes risk faster across more stakeholders.

The Financial Model Lies First

One of the earliest warning signals in troubled renewable projects is a financial model that continues to look healthy while the site reality deteriorates.

Financial models are inherently optimistic instruments.

They assume time behaves predictably. But execution does not follow spreadsheet logic.

A two-month delay in land handover does not simply shift commissioning by two months.

It cascades into

- Missed grid windows
- Re-sequenced construction

- Extended preliminaries
- Contractor claims
- Refinancing pressure
- Tax and regulatory exposure

The financial model lies first. The site reveals the truth later.

Execution leadership must learn to challenge financial optimism with operational realism.

The Unmanaged Interface Between Development and Delivery

In most renewable companies, development teams and execution teams operate as separate worlds.

Development teams close land, secure approvals, negotiate utilities and build feasibility.

Execution teams inherit whatever shape that feasibility takes.

But the handover between these two worlds is usually informal.

Critical assumptions rarely transfer clearly.

What was "manageable risk" during development becomes "execution nightmare" during delivery.

There is no structured institutional memory of

- What was compromised to close the deal
- What dependencies were deferred
- What uncertainties were consciously accepted

Projects do not suffer because people hide information.

They suffer because organizations do not create formal transition mechanisms.

The execution gap is often nothing more than a broken handover.

Schedules that are Built to Impress

Many renewable schedules are constructed backwards from the desired COD.

The milestone is fixed.

The activities are compressed.

The float quietly disappears.

The schedule becomes a sales document—not a delivery tool.

Real schedules must be built forward from readiness.

Not from regulatory deadlines.

Not from commercial commitments.

Not from investor expectations.

From physical, institutional and contractual reality.

When teams are forced to protect unrealistic schedules, truth disappears from reporting.

Progress is declared instead of measured.

Execution failure begins when schedules are defended instead of questioned.

Progress Reporting is Not Control

A large portion of project governance is spent reviewing progress.

Percentages.

Dashboards.

Heat maps.

But progress reporting only tells you what has already happened.

Execution control focuses on what is about to break.

Leading indicators matter more than lagging ones

- Unresolved land parcels in upcoming work zones
- Pending interface drawings

- Unapproved method statements
- Incomplete utility coordination
- Delayed advance payments to subcontractors

If leadership reviews focus only on completed activities, execution problems mature quietly in the future window.

Projects rarely collapse in yesterday's data.

They collapse in tomorrow's readiness.

Why Escalation Fails in Real Organizations

Most project organizations claim to encourage escalation.

In practice, escalation is culturally punished.

It is perceived as incompetence.

It is associated with personal failure.

It disrupts leadership comfort.

So teams soften messages.

They postpone bad news.

They attempt local fixes beyond their authority.

By the time escalation finally reaches senior leadership, optionality has already disappeared.

Execution maturity is not measured by how few issues are escalated.

It is measured by how early they are escalated.

The Lonely Position of the Project Leader

The execution gap exists largely because the project leader rarely controls the levers required to close it.

The project leader is accountable for delivery—but not for

- Land closure speed
- Approval prioritization
- Procurement policy exceptions

- Finance release timing
- Internal resource allocation

Authority is fragmented.

Accountability is centralized.

This structural imbalance is one of the deepest design flaws in renewable organizations.

True execution leadership requires

- Cross-functional authority
- Budgetary flexibility within limits
- Direct access to decision forums
- Power to stop activities that violate readiness gates

Without this, project leaders become coordinators—not delivery owners.

And coordination cannot replace authority.

India's Unique Execution Reality

In India, the execution gap widens further because many dependencies sit outside organizational control.

District administration.

State utilities.

Forest departments.

Local communities.

Political timing.

Festivals.

Weather windows.

These are not abnormal disturbances.

They are permanent features of the delivery environment.

Execution planning that assumes stable institutional timelines is not optimistic.

It is negligent.

Indian renewable execution requires contingency design, not contingency hope.

The Point of No Return

Every project has a moment when recovery becomes structurally impossible.

Not financially impossible.

Structurally impossible.

This usually occurs when

- Procurement commitments exceed site readiness
- Contractor mobilisation exceeds land availability
- Financing drawdowns exceed physical progress certainty

From this point onward, leadership loses flexibility.

Decisions become defensive.

Costs become sunk.

Schedules become symbolic.

Most leadership teams realize this point only in hindsight.

Execution discipline is about never crossing it.

From Vision to Commissioning Requires Architecture

The execution gap is not closed by motivation.

It is closed by architecture.

Clear readiness definitions.

Formal handover mechanisms.

Real decision rights.

Escalation protection.

Interface governance.

Risk ownership.

These are organizational design choices.

Not project tools.

Until renewable companies design their delivery organizations with the same rigor they apply to plant layouts, execution will remain vulnerable to personality, pressure and politics.

Closing Perspective

The journey from vision to commissioning is not a straight line. It is a fragile network of interdependent commitments.

Every weak interface becomes a future delay.

Every optimistic assumption becomes a future negotiation.

Every undefined authority becomes a future crisis.

The most dangerous space in a renewable project is not physical. It is organizational.

Between ambition and execution capability.

Between promise and readiness.

Between confidence and control.

If Chapter 1 exposed why technology is not the limiting factor, this chapter exposes a deeper reality:

Most renewable projects do not fail because they are difficult to build.

They fail because they are insufficiently designed to be delivered.

Chapter - 3

Land - The First Silent Risk

Before There is Power, There is Land.

No renewable energy project truly begins with a turbine or a solar module.

It begins with land.

And yet, land is often treated as a preliminary task—something to be "managed" while real work moves ahead.

In reality, land is the foundation risk upon which every other decision rests.

In the Indian renewable context, land is not just a physical asset. It is social, political, emotional, and legal terrain rolled into one.

Ignore this reality, and the project will pay the price—slowly, expensively, and publicly.

The Illusion of Land Availability

On spreadsheets, land is binary: Available or not available - Acquired or not acquired.

On the ground, land exists in shades of uncertainty.

A parcel may be identified but not agreed. A consent may be verbal but not documented. A mutation may be filed but not recorded. A farmer may agree today and reconsider tomorrow.

When leadership treats these shades as black-and-white certainty, execution risk quietly enters the project.

Why Land Delays are Rarely Sudden

Land does not usually derail projects overnight. It erodes confidence gradually.

A missing parcel forces layout changes. Layout changes trigger redesigns. Redesigns delay approvals. Delays push construction into the wrong season.

By the time the delay is acknowledged, the cost is already sunk.

Land risk compounds. It never stays isolated.

The Human Factor Nobody Models.

Land acquisition models account for price.

They rarely account for people.

In India, land ownership is often fragmented across families. Emotional value exceeds market value. Multiple intermediaries influence decisions. Local politics can shift alignment overnight.

A project team may believe it has reached agreement, only to discover that one stakeholder was never truly aligned.

Land fails projects not because of greed—but because of misunderstanding human dynamics.

Speed vs. Sensitivity

Execution pressure often pushes teams to accelerate land closure.

This is where mistakes happen.

Rushing land agreements creates: Legal vulnerabilities - Community resistance - Long-term reputational damage

Experienced project leaders know this paradox

The faster you try to close land without trust, the slower the project ultimately moves.

Sensitivity is not softness. It is execution intelligence.

The Cost of Partial Land Readiness

One of the most dangerous assumptions in renewables is

"We will start with available land and close the balance in parallel."

Partial land readiness creates fragmented construction fronts, inefficient mobilization, and constant replanning.

Contractors lose rhythm. Teams lose morale. Schedules lose credibility.

From an execution standpoint, 90% land readiness is closer to failure than success.

My Field Lesson

I once reviewed a project that was technically ready, financially approved, and EPC-aligned—yet stalled for months.

The reason was deceptively simple: two small land parcels.

Those parcels forced redesigns, delayed evacuation alignment, and triggered disputes that consumed leadership bandwidth.

The lesson was clear

Land risk ignored early will demand attention later—at a far higher cost.

Designing Land into Execution Planning

Execution-mature organizations treat land as a core execution stream, not a preliminary activity.

They ensure

- Clear land readiness gates before EPC mobilization
- Single-point accountability for land closure
- Continuous stakeholder engagement, not transactional negotiation
- Buffer timelines that reflect reality, not optimism

Land certainty creates execution confidence.

Land is Not a Task. It is a Commitment

Land reflects how seriously an organization respects execution reality.

If land is weak, everything above it is unstable.

In renewable projects, turbines can be replaced. Modules can be upgraded. Timelines can be revised.

Land disputes, once triggered, rarely resolve quietly.

That is why land is the first silent risk—and often the loudest failure.

The next chapter will address what happens after land is secured but power still cannot move: evacuation.

Because owning land is not enough.

Energy must still find a way out.

Land is an Execution System, Not a Real-Estate Activity

One of the most persistent structural mistakes in renewable organizations is where land sits inside the company.

It is often parked under administration, liaison, or "local support."

But land is not support.

Land is delivery infrastructure.

The quality of land work determines

- Whether layouts stabilize early
- Whether evacuation routes remain viable
- Whether construction sequencing remains continuous
- Whether local access remains uninterrupted

If land is managed as a transactional function, execution will inherit instability.

Land must be governed with the same seriousness as engineering or project controls.

The Myth of "We Have a Strong Local Agent"

Many project teams place enormous confidence in local intermediaries.

The logic is simple

"They understand the villagers."

"They have handled land before."

"They will manage resistance."

Local agents are valuable.

But they cannot replace organizational responsibility.

When land strategy is outsourced entirely to intermediaries, three blind spots emerge

- The project team loses visibility into real stakeholder sentiment
- Escalation pathways disappear
- Legal and social risks remain filtered through commercial optimism

By the time the developer hears about a brewing conflict, the narrative is already polarized.

Execution-mature organizations treat intermediaries as facilitators, not shields.

Ownership of land risk must remain firmly inside the developer's leadership structure.

Social Access is More Fragile than Legal Access

Most land dashboards track

- Agreements signed
- Payments released
- Registrations completed

Very few track

- Actual site access continuity
- Community acceptance levels
- Unresolved emotional or family disputes

In Indian renewable projects, site access can be withdrawn even after legal completion.

A locked gate does not violate a contract.

But it can stop a project.

This is the part of land risk that spreadsheets cannot capture.

Social access must be earned continuously—not secured once.

The Hidden Dependency: Local Power Structures

Every project site has invisible power structures.

Village leadership.

Informal brokers.

Political influencers.

Community elders.

Farmer unions.

These actors are rarely listed in stakeholder registers.

But they influence

- Whether equipment can move freely
- Whether construction teams feel safe
- Whether disputes escalate quietly or publicly

Land execution fails not because documents are missing, but because influence networks were ignored.

Ignoring local power structures does not make projects neutral.

It makes them vulnerable.

Why Layout Design Should Not Lead Land Closure

Many projects freeze layouts before land closure is fully secured.

This reverses execution logic.

Layouts should emerge from confirmed land—not aspirations of land.

When layouts drive land acquisition, teams create avoidable pressure points

- Forced negotiations on critical parcels
- Inflated expectations among landowners
- Reduced design flexibility later

Execution-mature projects allow layout adaptability during land consolidation and only freeze design once closure certainty is achieved.

Design discipline begins with land realism.

Land and Evacuation are a Single Risk System

One of the most underestimated interfaces in renewable projects is between land and evacuation.

Transmission lines, pooling substations, approach roads, cable routes—each has its own land footprint.

Projects often secure generation land first and treat evacuation land later.

This sequencing is dangerous.

Evacuation alignment changes can invalidate

- Tower positions
- Cable trenching plans
- Substation orientation
- Statutory approvals

A project can own its generation land and still be completely blocked by evacuation land disputes.

Land closure must be planned as a unified physical corridor—from generation to grid.

The Compounding Effect of Seasonal Windows

Land delays rarely exist in isolation.

They interact directly with weather windows.

In many regions of India

- Monsoon makes earthwork impossible
- Harvest seasons restrict farmer availability
- Festivals and elections disrupt negotiations

A two-week land delay before monsoon can become a four-month execution delay.

Land readiness must be measured not only against project schedules—but against seasonal realities.

This dimension is frequently ignored in centralized planning.

Legal Due Diligence is Necessary—but Not Sufficient

Most renewable developers have improved their legal due diligence significantly.

Title verification.

Encumbrance checks.

Litigation screening.

These are critical.

But legal clarity does not guarantee operational clarity.

Common execution failures still occur due to

- Internal family arrangements not reflected in records
- Informal inheritance understandings
- Pending partitions not yet legally filed
- Historical access rights not documented

Execution leadership must ask an uncomfortable question

"Who might object later—even if the law supports us today?"

This question protects projects more than any legal certificate.

The Psychological Fatigue of Prolonged Land Closure

Land acquisition is emotionally draining work.

It involves repeated conversations, conflict resolution, disappointment, negotiation and local pressure.

When land teams are overextended or under-resourced, two dangerous patterns appear

- Premature closure to meet targets
- Silent tolerance of unresolved risks

Land fatigue creates execution shortcuts.

Organizations that scale rapidly without strengthening land capacity unknowingly plant future disputes into their portfolios.

Land excellence is not built through deal-making skills alone.

It requires resilience, emotional intelligence and institutional backing.

When Leadership Engages Too Late

In many projects, senior leadership becomes involved in land only when escalation is unavoidable.

By then

- Positions have hardened
- Trust has eroded
- Narratives have polarized

Early leadership presence changes the tone of negotiations.

Not because of authority—but because of respect.

In sensitive land contexts, senior engagement communicates seriousness, stability and accountability.

Delegation without visibility weakens negotiating credibility.

Land Closure is a Reputational Event

Every land transaction becomes part of the developer's local reputation.

Farmers talk.

Communities compare experiences.

Future sites remember past behaviour.

Developers often underestimate how quickly reputational capital accumulates—or erodes—across districts.

One poorly handled project can raise resistance across an entire region.

Execution leadership must view land closure not as isolated deals—but as long-term relationship investments.

Building a Land Readiness Framework

Execution-mature organizations move beyond informal land tracking.

They define structured land readiness levels

- **Identification readiness** – parcels mapped, ownership understood
- **Consent readiness** – stakeholders aligned, social acceptance established
- **Legal readiness** – documentation complete, registrations defensible
- **Access readiness** – roads, entry points and movement rights secured
- **Interface readiness** – evacuation and infrastructure corridors aligned

Only when all five readiness layers are stable should construction sequencing be committed.

This discipline alone prevents a significant percentage of downstream delays.

The False Comfort of "We Will Handle It If It Comes"

Perhaps the most dangerous land-related phrase in project rooms is

"We will manage it if it comes up."

Land risk does not behave like a random event.

It behaves like delayed certainty.

What is ambiguous today will become visible later—under worse conditions.

Under tighter schedules.

Under higher cost pressure.

Under greater public exposure.

Execution maturity lies in converting ambiguity into clarity early—when solutions are still affordable.

Why Land is the First Test of Execution Culture

Land reveals the true execution culture of an organization.

It shows

- Whether realism is valued over optimism
- Whether patience is allowed under pressure
- Whether people are empowered to escalate early
- Whether leadership respects local complexity

Projects that treat land casually usually treat other execution risks the same way.

Land is simply the first place where this culture becomes visible.

Closing Reflection

Before power flows, before inverters synchronize, before commissioning ceremonies are planned, a much quieter and more fragile process decides the fate of the project.

Trust is built—or broken.

Communities are aligned—or alienated.

Access is protected—or contested.

Land is not only a legal boundary. It is a social contract between a project and its surroundings.

If this contract is weak, no amount of technical excellence can compensate for the disruption that follows.

That is why land is not just the first silent risk. It is the first integrity test of execution leadership.

And in the renewable transition India is undertaking at unprecedented scale, how we acquire land will matter as much as how much power we finally produce.

Chapter - 4

Evacuation - Power Without a Path

Generation is Pointless without Exit

Renewable energy projects celebrate capacity creation.

Megawatts are announced. Turbines are erected. Modules shimmer across landscapes.

But generation without evacuation is not progress.

It is stranded ambition.

In execution terms, evacuation is not an auxiliary activity—it is the exit strategy of the project. Without a clear, confirmed path to the grid, power has nowhere to go, revenues have nowhere to land, and confidence has nowhere to stand.

The Dangerous Assumption: "Grid Will Be Ready"

One of the most common—and costly—assumptions in renewable execution is that evacuation will somehow align itself with generation.

Teams rely on

- Verbal assurances
- Tentative letters
- Historical precedence

- Optimistic timelines

None of these evacuate power.

Grid readiness is not a sentiment. It is an engineered, approved, and commissioned reality.

Why Evacuation Fails Quietly

Evacuation rarely announces its failure early.

On paper, everything looks acceptable: Substations are "under development" - Transmission lines are "in progress" - Synchronization windows are "expected"

But evacuation slips in months, not days.

By the time generation assets are ready, evacuation gaps surface—and by then, options are limited and expensive.

Fragmented Ownership, Predictable Failure

Evacuation involves multiple entities: Project developers - Transmission utilities - State and central agencies - EPCs and OEMs

When ownership is fragmented, accountability dissolves.

Everyone is involved. No one is responsible.

Execution excellence demands a single-point evacuation owner who tracks approvals, construction, testing, and synchronization with the same rigor as generation.

The Timing Trap

Evacuation failures are often timing failures.

Generation construction follows predictable curves. Grid infrastructure does not.

Transmission work faces: Right-of-way challenges - Forest and railway crossings - Multi-agency approvals

When these realities are ignored in scheduling, evacuation becomes the bottleneck that no acceleration can fix.

Financial Impact of Idle Power

Idle power is invisible on construction dashboards—but painfully visible on balance sheets.

Every day of delayed evacuation means

- Lost revenue
- Interest accumulation
- Contractor claims
- Investor discomfort

In many Indian projects, evacuation delay has caused more financial damage than any equipment failure ever could.

My Execution Reality

I have seen projects where generation was completed proudly—only to wait months for grid connectivity.

Teams celebrated milestones while assets sat idle.

The lesson was sobering

Commissioning is not when machines start. It is when power flows and invoices follow.

Anything else is self-deception.

Designing Evacuation into the Project

Execution-mature organizations treat evacuation as a parallel critical path, not a downstream activity.

They ensure

- Firm evacuation approvals before major procurement
- Synchronization of transmission and generation schedules
- Contingency planning for grid delays
- Regular joint reviews with utilities

Evacuation certainty transforms project confidence.

Power Needs a Promise—and Proof

In renewable execution, belief does not move electrons.

Infrastructure does.

Promises do not evacuate power.

Planning does.

The next chapter will address what happens when land and evacuation are aligned—but execution still fails: governance versus firefighting.

Because even with a clear path out, projects can still collapse—if discipline is missing inside.

Generation without Exit Creates Strategic Risk, Not Just Delay

Evacuation failure is often discussed as a scheduling problem.

In reality, it is a strategic risk.

A project with stranded generation loses more than revenue.

It loses negotiating power—with lenders, with utilities, and with future partners.

Once a plant is mechanically complete and unable to evacuate power, the balance of leverage shifts immediately. The developer carries all the financial pressure. Every additional delay strengthens the position of everyone else in the system.

Evacuation weakness converts strong projects into fragile negotiations.

Evacuation is an Institutional Project, Not a Construction Activity

Developers frequently treat evacuation as a civil and electrical scope.

In practice, evacuation is an institutional delivery program.

It depends on

- Coordination between state and central transmission entities
- Synchronized planning between multiple project owners
- Regulatory approvals and statutory clearances

- Political and administrative timelines
- Regional grid strengthening programs

Construction is only the final visible layer.

The real work is institutional alignment.

Execution leadership must therefore manage evacuation like a multi-stakeholder program—not like an EPC package.

The Hidden Lag: Testing, Protection and Synchronization

One of the most underestimated phases in evacuation is not line completion or substation erection.

It is readiness for synchronization.

Projects routinely underestimate

- Protection scheme approvals
- Relay coordination studies
- Grid code compliance testing
- Joint inspections
- Energization permissions

Physically complete infrastructure does not mean grid-ready infrastructure.

Many projects enter mechanical completion with the false comfort that evacuation is "almost done," only to discover that formal synchronization windows are unavailable for weeks.

Evacuation readiness must include testing and protection approvals—not merely construction progress.

Shared Infrastructure Multiplies Execution Risk

Renewable parks and common pooling substations have improved infrastructure efficiency.

They have also multiplied governance complexity.

Shared evacuation creates

- Sequencing conflicts between multiple developers
- Disputes over readiness responsibility
- Misaligned construction priorities
- Coordination failures during testing and energization

Each developer controls its own generation assets.

No developer controls the shared system.

Without a formally empowered common evacuation authority, these projects drift into slow consensus-driven execution—exactly when speed is required.

Evacuation governance becomes the weakest link in otherwise well-built projects.

The Grid Does Not Care About Your Commercial Deadlines

Policy cut-offs, bidding milestones, tariff eligibility windows and commissioning incentives drive aggressive generation schedules.

The grid operates on an entirely different logic.

Grid planning is based on

- Regional load forecasts
- System stability requirements
- Outage planning cycles
- Long-term transmission expansion programs

Your project is one of many.

Execution failure often begins when project teams assume the grid will realign itself to project urgency.

It will not.

Grid readiness must be aligned early into utility planning cycles—not chased later through follow-ups and escalation.

ROW is Land Risk—Rebranded

Right-of-way challenges in transmission are frequently discussed as technical or legal obstacles.

In reality, ROW is land risk expressed at a larger, more political scale.

Transmission corridors cross

- Multiple villages
- Forest zones
- Highways and railways
- Private and community lands

Each crossing introduces

- Consent challenges
- Compensation negotiations
- Administrative approvals
- Litigation exposure

ROW complexity grows exponentially with corridor length.

Developers who underestimate ROW timelines inevitably overestimate evacuation certainty.

Why EPC Acceleration Cannot Save Evacuation Delays

When evacuation delays surface, leadership instinctively pushes EPC acceleration.

Additional manpower.

Extended shifts.

Compressed work fronts.

This response rarely helps.

Evacuation delays are rarely driven by construction productivity.

They are driven by

- Missing approvals
- Unavailable shutdown windows
- Incomplete protection approvals
- Unresolved interface disputes

Execution leadership must recognize when acceleration is ineffective—and focus instead on institutional resolution.

Field speed cannot overcome administrative latency.

The Cost Nobody Budgets: Seasonal Generation Loss

Idle generation during high resource seasons creates irreversible loss.

In wind projects, one lost wind season cannot be recovered later.

In solar projects, high irradiation months matter disproportionately to annual yield.

Financial models typically treat delayed commissioning as a timing issue.

In reality, it is often a volume issue.

Lost seasonal generation permanently alters cash flow curves.

This effect is rarely captured accurately in early project risk analysis.

Evacuation delay is therefore not just a timing risk—it is a performance risk.

The Psychological Trap of "Mechanical Completion"

Mechanical completion creates a dangerous psychological milestone.

Teams feel the project is almost over.

Leadership shifts attention to the next site.

Contractors begin demobilization.

But evacuation execution often intensifies after mechanical completion.

Testing.

Rectifications.

Interface coordination.

Joint inspections.

Projects that emotionally close too early lose execution focus when it is still required.

Execution maturity means treating evacuation completion—not mechanical completion—as the true finish line.

Why Developers Must Own Evacuation Even When They Do Not Build It

A dangerous misconception persists in many organizations

"Evacuation is utility responsibility."

Operationally, this may be correct.

Execution-wise, it is irrelevant.

The developer carries the revenue risk.

The developer carries the debt.

The developer carries investor exposure.

Ownership follows consequence—not contract.

Execution-mature developers therefore create internal evacuation leadership even when physical work is done by external agencies.

They track

- Statutory approvals
- Contractor progress of utilities
- Interface schedules
- Testing readiness
- Energization planning

Evacuation must be governed with the same discipline as any internal work package.

Early Warning Signals of Evacuation Failure

Evacuation failure is rarely sudden.

Warning signs appear early

- Protection scheme approvals slipping without clear recovery plans
- Utility meetings postponed repeatedly
- Transmission contractors demobilizing temporarily

- Row disputes escalating locally
- Synchronization windows discussed vaguely

Execution leadership must train teams to recognize evacuation risk indicators—not just construction delays.

The cost of ignoring early warnings is almost always higher than the cost of early intervention.

Evacuation Readiness Gates

Execution-mature projects define formal evacuation readiness gates.

Typical gates include

- All statutory and technical approvals obtained
- ROW secured for entire evacuation corridor
- Substation equipment delivered and installed
- Protection and communication systems tested
- Synchronization windows formally confirmed

Only after these gates are passed should

- Generation EPC acceleration be authorized
- Turbine erection peaks be scheduled
- Final module commissioning waves be launched

Without such gates, generation and evacuation drift apart.

Institutional Memory: Why the Same Mistakes Repeat

One of the quiet reasons evacuation failures keep recurring is organizational amnesia.

Each project treats its evacuation issues as unique.

In reality, most failures follow predictable patterns

- Approval sequencing errors
- Interface misalignment
- Utility planning mismatch

- ROW underestimation

But few organizations build structured evacuation post-mortems into their delivery systems.

Execution excellence requires institutional learning—not heroic recovery.

India's Grid is Strengthening—But So are Expectations

India's transmission infrastructure is improving rapidly.

But expectations from utilities are also rising.

Grid code compliance, protection coordination, cybersecurity requirements and real-time monitoring expectations are increasing.

Evacuation complexity is therefore not reducing.

It is evolving.

Execution leadership must invest in internal grid interface capability—not treat evacuation as an external technical speciality.

Closing Reflection

Generation capacity can be created by contractors.

Evacuation certainty must be created by leadership.

It demands early institutional engagement, disciplined governance, and relentless follow-up across organizational boundaries.

The renewable transition will not be slowed by lack of technology.

It will be slowed by lack of exit readiness.

Until developers treat evacuation as a core strategic capability—equal in importance to land and construction—stranded assets will remain an uncomfortable feature of otherwise impressive portfolios.

Because in renewable execution, power is not created when turbines turn.

Power is created only when the grid is ready to receive it.

Chapter - 5

Governance vs. Firefighting

When Foundations Exist but Projects Still Fail

By this stage, a renewable project may appear safe.

Land is largely secured. Evacuation is approved. Technology is mobilized.

And yet—this is often where execution begins to unravel.

The reason is not technical. It is not regulatory.

It is governance failure.

Projects do not collapse because problems appear. They collapse because organizations respond to problems without structure.

The Illusion of Control

Many leadership teams believe they are governing projects because

- Review meetings are frequent
- Dashboards are updated
- Escalations are loud

In reality, what they are practicing is firefighting, not governance.

Firefighting reacts to symptoms. Governance controls causes.

One creates urgency. The other creates stability.

What Governance Actually Means in Execution

Governance is not bureaucracy.

Governance is clarity.

It defines: Who decides - Who owns risk - Who escalates - Who absorbs impact

In execution-mature organizations, governance ensures that decisions are taken before crises emerge—not after.

How Firefighting Becomes the Default Culture

Firefighting rarely starts intentionally.

It emerges when: Timelines are unrealistic - Dependencies are ignored - Accountability is diffused - Leaders reward speed over discipline

Over time, teams stop planning and start reacting.

Urgency replaces thinking. Pressure replaces process.

This culture feels heroic—but it is unsustainable.

The Cost of Permanent Urgency

Projects run in firefighting mode suffer predictable consequences

- Exhausted teams
- Inconsistent decisions
- Vendor mistrust
- Quality compromises

Most dangerously, firefighting normalizes deviation.

Missed milestones become acceptable. Temporary fixes become permanent.

Execution discipline quietly erodes.

My Uncomfortable Observation

I have watched capable teams fail—not because they lacked talent, but because leadership systems collapsed under pressure.

Decisions were delayed to avoid conflict. Escalations were softened to preserve optimism.

The result was chaos disguised as effort.

The hard truth is this

Leadership tolerance defines execution standards.

Governance is a Design Choice

Strong governance does not emerge during crisis.

It is designed early and defended consistently.

Execution-focused organizations establish

- Clear escalation matrices
- Decision timelines
- Authority boundaries
- Risk ownership registers

These mechanisms reduce noise and protect momentum.

The Single-Point Leadership Principle

One of the most common governance failures in renewable projects is shared ownership.

Multiple leaders, overlapping authority, and unclear decision rights create paralysis.

Execution requires one accountable owner.

Collaboration is essential—but accountability must be singular.

From Firefighting to Flow

Projects that transition from firefighting to flow do not eliminate problems.

They manage them predictably.

Governance provides rhythm.

It allows teams to anticipate issues, absorb shocks, and maintain credibility.

Discipline is a Leadership Choice

Firefighting feels active. Governance feels restrictive.

But only one delivers projects.

As renewable projects grow larger and more complex, leadership systems must mature faster than ambition.

Because even with land secured and evacuation ready, projects will fail—

Not when problems arise,

But when governance gives way to chaos.

The next chapter will examine the silent killer that thrives inside weak governance systems: poor coordination.

Governance is a Behavior System, Not an Organization Chart

Most renewable companies believe governance lives in structure.

Project committees.

Steering groups.

Escalation ladders.

But governance does not fail because boxes are missing on charts.

- It fails because daily behavior is not aligned to those boxes.
- If a project manager must bypass the defined authority path to get work done, governance has already collapsed.
- If decisions depend on who shouts the loudest rather than who owns the risk, governance has already collapsed.
- If escalation is treated as weakness instead of responsibility, governance has already collapsed.

Execution governance is a behaviour system.

It survives only when leaders repeatedly demonstrate that rules apply even under pressure.

The Silent Killer: Decision Avoidance

Firefighting cultures are not created by fast decisions.

They are created by avoided decisions.

In renewable execution, the most damaging delays are not construction delays.

They are decision delays.

Scope clarifications.

Contractual interpretations.

Design freezes.

Interface responsibilities.

Payment approvals.

When leaders postpone uncomfortable calls, teams continue working in uncertainty.

That uncertainty later converts into claims, rework and conflict.

In many projects I have reviewed, months of site disruption could be traced back to one deferred leadership decision.

Governance is not about deciding correctly.

It is about deciding early—while options still exist.

Why Committees Cannot Replace Accountability

Committees feel safe.

They distribute responsibility.

They dilute conflict.

They protect individuals.

They also destroy execution velocity.

Committees are effective for policy and strategy.

They are dangerous for live delivery environments.

Execution requires accountable leadership—not collective comfort.

Every unresolved interface issue sitting in a committee agenda is usually owned by no one in reality.

When accountability becomes shared, consequences become orphaned.

Governance Protects People—Firefighting Uses Them

Firefighting cultures consume their best people first.

High performers are repeatedly pulled into crisis resolution.

They become informal integrators of broken systems.

They absorb conflict that governance should have resolved.

Over time, the organization becomes dependent on individuals instead of systems.

This is one of the clearest signals of governance weakness:

Projects survive because of people—not because of process.

When those people leave, execution collapses instantly.

Strong governance protects talent by removing the need for heroics.

The Link between Governance and Trust

Contractors do not trust organizations.

They trust predictability.

They watch

- How fast decisions are taken
- Whether approvals are reversed later
- Whether commitments survive leadership changes
- Whether escalation leads to clarity or politics

In weak governance environments, contractors hedge.

They slow down.

They inflate risk premiums.

They protect cash flow aggressively.

Execution cost rises not because contractors are inefficient—but because governance is unreliable.

Trust is not created by relationships alone.

It is created by consistent governance behavior.

Governance Must Be Visible at Site Level

One of the biggest mistakes leadership teams make is assuming governance is only needed at the top.

In reality, site teams experience governance—or its absence—every day.

They experience it when

- Drawings change without explanation
- Priorities change without authority
- Instructions conflict between departments
- Approvals take weeks without feedback

When governance is unclear at site level, execution reality is improvised.

No amount of executive steering can repair daily operational ambiguity.

Governance must travel downward—not remain trapped in boardrooms.

The Real Transition: From Control to Confidence

Firefighting leaders try to control execution.

Governance leaders build confidence in execution systems.

Control creates dependence.

Confidence creates resilience.

The real purpose of governance is not to reduce risk to zero.

It is to make risk manageable, visible and owned.

Projects that are governed well do not feel slower.

They feel calmer.

And calm execution is not a luxury in renewable delivery.

It is a competitive advantage.

Final Thought for this Chapter

Technology will continue to evolve.

Land and evacuation challenges will remain complex.

Schedules will always be aggressive.

But only one variable is fully within leadership control: the way decisions are made, owned and protected.

Firefighting makes leaders visible.

Governance makes organizations reliable.

And in the renewable energy sector that is now building national infrastructure—not experimental assets—reliability is the only leadership legacy that truly matters.

Chapter - 6

The Cost of Poor Coordination

When Everyone is Busy but Nothing Moves.

In renewable energy projects, delays rarely come from inactivity.

They come from misaligned activity.

Land teams are negotiating. Engineers are designing.

EPCs are mobilizing. Finance is tracking cash flows.

Everyone is working.

And yet—the project stalls.

This is the hidden cost of poor coordination: progress in silos that does not translate into progress on ground.

Coordination is Not Communication

Many organizations confuse coordination with communication.

Emails are exchanged. Calls are made. Meetings are held.

But coordination is not about information flow.

Coordination is about timing, sequence, and dependency alignment.

A drawing issued too early is as damaging as a drawing issued too late. A payment released out of sequence creates as much risk as a delayed one.

Execution breaks not when people don't talk—but when actions are not synchronized.

The Invisible Cost Centre

Poor coordination rarely appears as a line item in project budgets.

Instead, it shows up as

- Idle manpower
- Re-mobilization costs
- Rework and redesign
- Claims and counterclaims
- Lost credibility with contractors

These costs are scattered, justified, and normalized.

By the time leadership realizes the impact, margins are already eroded.

Land vs EPC: A Familiar Collision

One of the most common coordination failures occurs between land teams and EPC execution.

Land closure timelines slip quietly. EPC schedules move ahead optimistically.

When the two finally collide, construction fronts disappear overnight.

EPCs blame land. Land teams blame pressure.

The project pays the price.

Coordination failure does not require incompetence—only optimism without integration.

Engineering vs. Site Reality

Design teams often work in controlled environments, far from site realities.

Layouts assume access roads. Foundations assume soil uniformity. Cable routes assume continuity.

Site teams discover constraints too late.

When engineering and site execution are not tightly coordinated, projects suffer repeated micro-delays that compound into macro failures.

Finance as a Bottleneck—or an Enabler

Finance teams are often brought in late—as controllers, not partners.

Payment cycles misaligned with site progress choke contractors. Cash releases without readiness encourage premature mobilization.

In execution-mature projects, finance is a coordination function, not just a compliance one.

Cash flow timing is as critical as material delivery.

My Pattern Recognition

Across projects, I have seen the same pattern repeat

- Each function optimizes its own success
- No one optimizes the project's flow

This is not a people problem.

It is a system design failure.

Projects don't fail because teams are weak. They fail because coordination is optional.

Coordination Requires Ownership

Coordination does not happen by consensus.

It requires ownership.

An empowered project leader must: Align timelines across functions - Enforce readiness gates - Stop premature actions - Resolve dependency conflicts early

Without this authority, coordination becomes negotiation—and execution slows.

Designing for Flow

High-performing renewable projects are designed for flow, not speed.

They

- Sequence activities deliberately
- Limit parallel work until readiness is proven
- Measure progress by completed interfaces, not activity volume

Flow creates predictability. Predictability creates confidence.

The Real Cost

Poor coordination does not announce itself as failure.

It erodes margins. It stretches timelines. It exhausts teams.

By the time it is visible, recovery is expensive.

The next chapter will address the most underestimated factor behind coordination failure: ***people capability and accountability.***

Because systems only work when the people inside them are prepared to own outcomes.

Coordination Breaks at Interfaces, Not Inside Functions

Most renewable organizations attempt to improve coordination by strengthening individual departments.

Better land processes.

Better engineering controls.

Better EPC management.

Better finance approvals.

But coordination failure rarely originates inside a function.

It appears at interfaces.

Between land and engineering.

Between engineering and procurement.

Between procurement and site execution.

Between site progress and finance release.

Between evacuation planning and commissioning readiness.

Each interface is a risk handover point.

When interfaces are not explicitly owned, responsibility dissolves into conversation.

The project does not slow down because people are careless.

It slows down because no one is accountable for what passes between teams.

The Missing Role: Interface Ownership

One of the most underdeveloped roles in renewable project organizations is the interface owner.

An interface owner is not a coordinator.

He or she is accountable for ensuring that two dependent streams move together.

For example

- Land access versus foundation start
- Drawing freeze versus procurement release
- Inverter delivery versus substation readiness
- Turbine erection versus crane mobilization
- Site progress versus billing readiness

Without named interface owners, coordination depends on personal relationships and informal follow-ups.

That is not a system.

That is a vulnerability.

Coordination Fails First Under Pressure

During normal execution, coordination gaps can be absorbed quietly.

Under schedule pressure, they surface brutally.

When timelines tighten

- Land teams protect closure numbers
- Engineering teams protect issue dates
- Procurement teams protect purchase orders
- Site teams protect daily progress

Each function protects its own performance metric.

The project's flow becomes secondary.

This is why coordination collapses precisely when projects enter critical phases.

Execution systems that rely on goodwill do not survive pressure.

Only role clarity and authority do.

Progress Metrics Hide Coordination Debt

Most project dashboards track activity completion.

Drawings issued.

Modules delivered.

Foundations cast.

Towers erected.

Very few dashboards track interface readiness.

Was access available when foundations started?

Was evacuation alignment frozen when procurement advanced?

Was payment released when site productivity peaked?

Coordination debt accumulates quietly when activity metrics replace flow metrics.

The project looks busy.

The interfaces are broken.

Why Coordination Cannot Be Delegated

Many leaders assume coordination is the project manager's responsibility.

In practice, coordination authority must be supported by leadership behavior.

- If a project leader cannot stop procurement when engineering is unstable.
- If a project leader cannot delay mobilization when land access is weak.
- If a project leader cannot challenge finance when payment timing hurts execution.

Coordination becomes symbolic.

Ownership without authority produces frustration—not flow.

The India Reality: More Stakeholders, More Interfaces

In Indian renewable projects, coordination complexity multiplies because

- Land involves multiple families and intermediaries
- Utilities involve several departments and approval layers
- Contractors operate through local subcontractors
- Administration interacts with district-level systems

Every additional stakeholder introduces new interfaces.

Execution leadership in India must therefore design coordination intentionally.

Not hope for it.

Coordination is a Leadership Discipline

The most effective project leaders I have worked with are not the best communicators.

They are the best integrators.

They relentlessly ask

"What will break if this moves ahead today?"

"Who is not ready for this decision?"

"What dependency are we ignoring?"

They protect sequence more aggressively than speed.

This is not an operational detail.

This is execution leadership.

Closing Reflection

Poor coordination is not an accident.

It is the predictable outcome of organizations that are built around functions instead of flow.

Renewable projects succeed when

- Interfaces are visible
- Dependencies are owned
- Sequencing is protected
- Authority supports integration

Without this, even the best land strategy, strongest EPC, and most advanced technology cannot create momentum.

Because in execution, movement is not created by effort.

It is created by alignment.

Chapter - 7

People, Not PowerPoint

Execution is a Human Discipline

Renewable energy organizations invest heavily in frameworks.

Process maps. Dashboards. MIS formats. Review decks.

Yet projects continue to fail.

The uncomfortable truth is this

Execution maturity is not built on PowerPoint. It is built on people.

No framework survives weak ownership. No dashboard compensates for indecision. No process delivers results if the people executing it lack clarity, capability, or courage.

The Skill Gap Nobody Wants to Admit

The renewable sector has grown faster than its talent base.

Projects scaled from tens of megawatts to hundreds.

Complexity multiplied. Interfaces exploded.

But people development did not keep pace.

Many project leaders today are technically strong but execution-light

- Comfortable reporting progress
- Less comfortable owning outcomes
- Skilled at escalation, not resolution

Execution requires a different muscle—one built through accountability, not experience alone.

When Roles Exist but Ownership Does Not

Most organizations have clearly defined roles.

What they lack is ownership.

Ownership is not a designation. It is a mindset.

An owner does not say

> "This is not my scope."

An owner asks

> "What must I do to ensure this does not fail?"

Projects fail when roles are clear but ownership is missing.

Accountability vs Blame

In weak execution cultures, accountability is confused with blame.

People avoid decisions to avoid consequences.

Execution slows.

In strong cultures, accountability is safety.

People take decisions knowing leadership will support intent—even if outcomes need correction.

Fear kills execution faster than incompetence.

The Reporting Trap

Many professionals are promoted for their ability to present information.

Few are evaluated on their ability to resolve issues.

As a result

- Problems are reported repeatedly
- Decisions are deferred politely
- Ownership diffuses quietly

Execution leadership is not about visibility.

It is about closure.

My Realization

Early in my career, I believed strong systems would force execution discipline.

They did not.

What changed outcomes was placing the right people in the right roles—and backing them decisively.

Execution improves when leaders stop asking

> “Why is this delayed?”

And start asking

> “Who owns this—and what support do they need to close it?”

Capability is Contextual

A good engineer does not automatically become a good project leader.

Execution roles require

- Decision-making under ambiguity
- Stakeholder management
- Risk ownership
- Financial awareness

Without deliberate capability building, organizations promote technical experts into roles they were never prepared for.

This is not a people failure.

It is a leadership design failure.

Building Execution Leaders

Execution-mature organizations invest intentionally in people.

They

- Define clear ownership boundaries
- Train decision
- making, not just tools
- Reward closure over activity
- Protect accountable leaders from political fallout

People rise to the standards they are protected by.

Why Frameworks Still Matter—but Second

Frameworks are important.

They provide structure.

But they only work when people

- Respect them
- Understand their intent
- Have the authority to enforce them

Without people's maturity, frameworks become theater.

The Execution Equation

Execution excellence follows a simple equation

Capability* × *Ownership* × *Accountability = Results

Remove any one factor—and the system collapses.

People Decide the Energy Transition.

Technology will evolve. Policies will change. Markets will fluctuate.

But projects will always be delivered by people.

If renewable energy is to scale reliably, organizations must mature their people faster than their capacity targets.

Because in the end, turbines don't commission projects.

People do.

The next chapter will explore what happens when people are capable—but incentives are misaligned: execution versus contracts.

The Myth of "We Have Good People"

One of the most common defences I hear in post-mortems is this

"We have good people. They are working very hard."

Both statements are often true.

And both are often irrelevant.

Execution does not fail because people are bad.

It fails because "good people" are placed inside weak execution environments.

Good people without authority hesitate.

Good people without protection escalate instead of deciding.

Good people without clarity optimize their comfort zone.

Organizations do not get execution outcomes from intentions.

They get outcomes from behavior—and behavior is shaped by system

Why Experience Alone Does Not Create Execution Strength

The renewable sector often equates experience with execution capability.

Years in industry.

Number of projects handled.

Installed capacity delivered.

But experience without reflection creates repetition, not mastery.

Many professionals carry forward habits that worked at smaller scale into projects that are fundamentally different in complexity.

What breaks is not competence—but adaptability.

Execution leadership requires unlearning as much as learning

- Unlearning escalation as default behavior
- Unlearning dependence on informal assurances
- Unlearning hero-based problem solving
- Unlearning tolerance for ambiguity

Without this, experience becomes a ceiling instead of an asset.

Execution is Emotional Work (And We Pretend it isn't)

Project execution is not only technical and managerial.

It is emotional.

Conflict with contractors.

Pressure from leadership.

Fear of failure.

Fatigue from constant urgency.

Loneliness of ownership.

Most organizations pretend these dynamics do not exist.

As a result, execution roles quietly burn people out.

When leaders ignore the emotional load of execution, three things happen:

Decision-making becomes defensive.

Ownership shrinks to formal scope.

Courage disappears from the system.

Execution maturity requires acknowledging that leadership under uncertainty is psychologically demanding—and designing support accordingly.

The Unspoken Contract between Leaders and Teams

Every execution role carries an unspoken contract.

It answers three questions in the mind of the person holding it

- If I take a decision and it fails, will I be supported?
- If I escalate early, will I be punished or trusted?
- If I push back on unrealistic expectations, will I be heard?

In weak cultures, the answers are unclear or negative.

So people protect themselves

- They delay decisions.
- They soften truths.
- They escalate defensively.

Execution slows—not because people don't care, but because they don't feel safe to own outcomes.

Leadership behaviour writes this contract every day.

When Talent Leaves, Execution Debt Surfaces

One of the most dangerous moments in a renewable organization is when a strong execution leader leaves.

If execution immediately collapses, it reveals an uncomfortable truth:

The system never worked.

The person was compensating for it.

Hero-dependent execution is fragile.

Scalable execution requires that

- Ownership is role-based, not personality-based
- Decision rights are institutional, not informal
- Authority is documented, not implied

People should strengthen systems—not replace them.

Why Training Programs Often Miss the Point

Most capability-building efforts in renewable companies focus on tools.

Primavera.

MS Project.

MIS formats.

Contract basics.

These are necessary—but insufficient.

Execution failure rarely happens because someone didn't know *how* to do something.

It happens because they didn't know *when* to decide, *what* to escalate, or *how* to own ambiguity.

What execution leaders truly need training in?

- Decision-making under incomplete information
- Prioritization under conflicting pressure
- Managing upward without fear
- Saying "no" when readiness is weak
- Holding others accountable without authority abuse

These are leadership muscles—not software skills.

Ownership without Span of Control is Cruel

One of the most damaging organizational practices is assigning ownership without control.

Project leaders held responsible for timelines they cannot influence.

Site heads accountable for payments they cannot approve.

Engineering managers blamed for changes driven by land uncertainty.

This creates learned helplessness.

People stop owning outcomes because ownership feels unfair.

Execution leadership must align three things

- Responsibility
- Authority
- Consequence

If anyone is missing, execution degrades.

Accountability Must Be Binary, Not Collective

In many execution reviews, accountability is described in plural.

"We need to fix this."

"The team should close this."

"We are responsible."

This language feels collaborative—but it is execution poison.

Accountability must be binary.

One issue.

One owner.

One closure date.

Support can be collective.

Ownership cannot.

Projects do not fail because people refuse responsibility.

They fail because responsibility is diluted beyond recognition.

The Difference between High Performers and Execution Leaders

High performers deliver tasks.

Execution leaders deliver outcomes.

High performers ask:

"What do I need to do?"

Execution leaders ask

"What must happen for this to succeed?"

This difference is subtle—but decisive.

Organizations that promote task excellence without testing outcome ownership eventually plateau in execution capability.

Leadership pipelines must reward

- Problem closure, not problem explanation
- Cross-functional ownership, not silo efficiency
- Uncomfortable truth-telling, not polished reporting

Why Incentives Shape Behaviour More than Vision

Many renewable organizations speak passionately about execution excellence.

Few align incentives accordingly.

People are rewarded for

- Starting fast
- Showing progress
- Meeting intermediate milestones

Rarely for

- Stopping premature mobilization
- Delaying commitments due to weak readiness
- Preventing future problems before they appear

As a result, smart professionals learn what the system truly values.

They optimize for optics, not outcomes.

Execution excellence requires incentive courage—rewarding prevention, not just activity.

The Leadership Shift That Changes Everything

At some point, leadership must shift its core question.

From

"Why is this not moving faster?"

To

"What decision is pending that is blocking flow?"

This single shift transforms conversations.

It forces clarity.

It exposes ownership gaps.

It moves attention from effort to constraint.

Execution accelerates not when people work harder—but when leaders remove decision bottlenecks.

Execution is a Moral Choice

This may sound uncomfortable, but it is true.

Execution quality reflects leadership values.

- Do we value truth over comfort?
- Do we protect owners or punish them?
- Do we prefer predictability or heroics?
- Do we design systems—or rely on people to suffer quietly?

Every delayed project carries these answers within it.

Execution is not only operational discipline.

It is organizational integrity in action.

Closing Reflection

PowerPoint can inspire alignment.

Frameworks can create structure.

Dashboards can provide visibility.

But none of them can replace courage, ownership, and accountability.

Renewable energy is no longer a niche industry experimenting with scale. It is building national infrastructure under public scrutiny, financial pressure, and policy urgency.

This demands a different standard of people leadership.

Not louder reviews.

Not smarter slides.

Not more complex processes.

But people who are

- Clear about ownership
- Supported in decision-making
- Protected when they act with integrity
- Held accountable with fairness

Because the future of renewable execution will not be decided by how well we plan.

It will be decided by how well our people are enabled to own reality—and act on it.

Chapter - 8

The Illusion of Urgency

Urgent Does Not Mean Important

In modern renewable projects, urgency has become a badge of commitment.

Messages are marked ***urgent***. Calls are made late at night. WhatsApp groups buzz relentlessly.

Activity increases.

Quality declines.

False urgency feels productive, but it quietly destroys execution discipline.

The Rise of WhatsApp Project Management

WhatsApp has become the unofficial control room of many projects.

Decisions are pushed in fragments. Context is lost in threads. Accountability diffuses across messages.

Speed replaces thinking.

Urgency without structure converts complex execution decisions into emotional reactions.

Deadline Theatrics

Artificial deadlines are announced to create pressure.

Teams respond by compressing logic instead of improving planning.

Buffers disappear. Risks are hidden.

Projects move faster—towards failure.

Urgency can move people. Only planning moves projects.

Why Leaders Create False Urgency

False urgency often comes from good intent

- Desire to show momentum
- Fear of missing targets
- Pressure from stakeholders

But intent does not neutralize impact.

Urgency shortcuts thinking.

The Cost of Continuous Pressure

Permanent urgency has predictable effects

- Burnout
- Poor decisions
- Quality compromise
- Loss of trust

Execution becomes reactive.

Calm is a Competitive Advantage

High-performing teams operate with urgency and calm.

They

- Protect planning time
- Escalate early
- Maintain buffers

Calm is not slow.

Calm is controlled speed.

My Hard Rule

Over time, I learned to distrust urgency that arrives without data.

If everything is urgent, nothing is.

Execution improves when leaders demand clarity before speed.

Designing Urgency That Works

Effective urgency

- Is linked to verified readiness
- Has a clear owner
- Respects execution sequence

Anything else is noise.

Urgency without Discipline is Chaos

Renewable projects do not fail due to lack of effort.

They fail when urgency replaces thinking.

The next chapter will explore how contracts and incentives often reinforce this behavior: Execution vs Contracts.

Urgency is a Signal, Not a Strategy

Urgency should tell leaders that something in the system is weak.

It should not become the system itself.

When leaders rely on urgency to move work forward, they are unknowingly admitting that planning, sequencing and ownership are insufficient.

Healthy execution systems reduce the need for urgency.

Unhealthy systems require urgency to survive.

This distinction matters.

If a project needs constant escalation, constant chasing and constant emotional pressure to progress, it is not moving fast.

It is compensating for missing structure.

The Real Enemy is Not Delay — It is Panic

There is a critical difference between time pressure and panic.

Time pressure is real.

Regulatory deadlines, grid windows and commercial milestones are unavoidable.

Panic is optional.

Panic enters execution when teams are surprised by predictable risks.

Land delays that were visible.

Evacuation approvals that were always uncertain.

Interface clashes that were never owned.

Payment cycles that were misaligned from the start.

False urgency is often nothing more than delayed realism.

Execution maturity is measured by how early leaders confront uncomfortable facts — not how loudly they react later.

Why Urgency Breaks Coordination First

Under urgency, coordination collapses before execution collapses.

Engineering releases drawings to meet a date, not readiness.

Procurement releases orders to show action, not stability.

Site teams mobilise to demonstrate effort, not access.

Each function protects its own optics.

Project flow disappears.

This is why urgency amplifies the very problems leaders are trying to solve.

When leaders demand speed without sequencing, they force functions to act independently — and independence is the opposite of coordination.

The Leadership Addiction to Visible Activity

One reason false urgency spreads so easily is because it creates visible movement.

Calls.

Messages.

Instructions.

Follow-ups.

Leadership feels involved.

Teams feel watched.

The organisation feels busy.

But visible activity is not execution progress.

Invisible readiness is.

Land access clarity.

Evacuation approval certainty.

Interface freeze.

Cash flow alignment.

Contractual risk closure.

These are quiet achievements.

They do not trend on WhatsApp groups.

But they decide project outcomes.

Strong execution leaders learn to value invisible work more than visible pressure.

The Discipline of Saying "Not Yet"

One of the hardest leadership skills in renewable execution is the ability to say:

"Not yet."

Not yet to mobilisation.

Not yet to parallel work.

Not yet to acceleration.

Not yet to public commitments.

This is not resistance.

It is responsibility.

Execution leaders protect sequence even when leadership pressure demands speed.

They understand that starting early on the wrong foundation creates more urgency later.

How to Replace Urgency with Control

Projects that successfully escape the urgency trap adopt three simple but powerful practices:

First, they define readiness gates.

No activity advances without clear entry criteria.

Second, they protect planning time.

Not as a formality, but as a decision-making space.

Third, they restrict communication channels for execution decisions.

Not everything belongs on WhatsApp.

Critical decisions require traceability, ownership and context.

Urgency fades naturally when structure appears.

A Personal Leadership Shift

One of the most valuable habits I developed over time was asking a single question whenever urgency appeared:

"What assumption just failed?"

Behind every urgent request lies a broken assumption.

A timeline that was unrealistic.

A dependency that was ignored.

A risk that was underestimated.

Fixing the assumption removes the urgency.

Ignoring it creates the next escalation.

Closing Reflection

Urgency is not leadership.

Clarity is.

Pressure does not create execution maturity.

Design does.

In renewable energy delivery, where projects are becoming larger, more interconnected and more publicly visible, leadership behaviour around urgency will increasingly determine organisational credibility.

Because teams can survive demanding schedules.

They cannot survive permanent panic.

And projects do not fail because leaders demanded speed.

They fail because leaders forgot that execution needs order before acceleration.

Chapter - 9

Risk Management – The Missing Discipline

Risks are Known. Ownership is Not.

In most renewable projects, risks are not invisible.

They are identified early. They are discussed in meetings. They are listed in registers.

And then—they are ignored.

Risk management fails not because risks are unknown, but because ***ownership is weak and discipline is absent.***

The Illusion of the Risk Register

Almost every project maintains a risk register.

It is created during planning. Updated during reviews. Shared during audits.

And rarely used to drive decisions.

Registers become documentation tools, not execution instruments.

A risk acknowledged but not acted upon is not management—it is delay with awareness.

Reactive Mitigation is Not Mitigation

In weak execution cultures, mitigation starts after impact.

Land disputes are handled after work stops. Evacuation delays are escalated after assets are idle. Contractor claims are negotiated after trust erodes.

This is reaction, not mitigation.

True risk management reduces probability *before* damage occurs.

Why Leaders Underestimate Risk

Risk discussions are uncomfortable.

They slow optimism. They challenge timelines. They demand buffers.

Under pressure, leaders unconsciously downplay risks to preserve momentum.

Momentum achieved by denial is temporary.

The Cost of Unowned Risk

Unowned risks behave predictably

- They age silently
- They compound across functions
- They surface simultaneously

When risks finally materialize, leaders ask

> "Why didn't anyone flag this earlier?"

The answer is usually uncomfortable:

It was flagged.

It just wasn't owned.

My Realization

Early in my leadership journey, I believed risk reviews were enough.

They were not.

What changed outcomes was assigning one clear owner per critical risk, with authority to act.

Execution improved when risk ownership became personal—not procedural.

Risk is a Leadership Conversation

Risk management is not a technical exercise.

It is a leadership discipline.

Strong leaders

- Encourage early risk disclosure
- Protect messengers, not silence them
- Act before certainty

Weak leaders reward optimism—and punish caution.

Designing a Living Risk System

Execution-mature organizations treat risk as dynamic.

They

- Review risks weekly, not quarterly
- Link risks to decisions, not reports
- Track mitigation effectiveness
- Close risks only after resolution, not explanation

Risk systems must influence execution—not decorate governance.

The False Comfort of Experience

Many teams rely on experience to manage risk.

Experience helps—but it also creates blind spots.

"We've handled this before."

Past survival is not future protection.

Each project introduces new combinations of risk.

Discipline Over Heroics

Projects with weak risk discipline celebrate heroics.

Projects with strong discipline prevent crises.

The difference is invisible—until it isn't.

Risk Decides Reliability

Technology determines possibility.

Execution determines delivery.

Risk management determines reliability.

Without disciplined risk ownership, renewable projects will continue to fail quietly—one ignored risk at a time.

The next chapter will examine how contracts and incentives often undermine even good risk discipline:

Execution vs. Contracts.

Risk Must Compete With Progress

One of the most uncomfortable realities of project execution is that risk management competes directly with visible progress.

Closing risks rarely looks productive.

It delays commitments.

It adds conditions.

It raises uncomfortable questions.

It slows decisions that would otherwise move forward quickly.

As a result, in many renewable projects, risk conversations are tolerated only until they start interfering with delivery promises.

Once pressure rises, risk becomes background noise.

Execution maturity is the ability to protect risk discipline even when momentum is politically and emotionally attractive.

The Real Failure is Not Missed Risks – It is Ignored Triggers

Most projects do not fail because risks were poorly identified.

They fail because early warning triggers were never defined.

A proper risk does not only have

- A description
- A probability
- An impact score

It must also have a trigger.

A clear observable signal that tells the team

"This risk is now moving from possibility to reality."

For example

- Land mutation not recorded within a defined time window
- Evacuation approval not issued by a committed milestone
- Vendor mobilization slipping beyond a threshold
- Payment cycle extending beyond agreed norms

Without triggers, teams argue about perception.

With triggers, teams act on evidence

Why Mitigation Plans Often Remain Theoretical

Many mitigation actions in renewable projects are written in vague language

"Follow up with authority."

"Engage stakeholders."

"Monitor progress closely."

These are not mitigation actions.

They are intentions.

A real mitigation action must answer three questions

Who will do it?

By when?

What will change if it succeeds?

If a mitigation action does not change a decision, a contract, a sequence, or a commitment, it is not mitigation.

It is documentation.

Risk Ownership without Decision Rights is Cosmetic

Assigning a risk owner is meaningless if the owner cannot influence outcomes.

If the person owning evacuation risk cannot engage the utility at leadership level…

If the person owning land risk cannot approve compensation revisions…

If the person owning contractor risk cannot adjust sequencing or scope…

Ownership becomes ceremonial.

Execution-mature organizations link every major risk to someone who can actually change the future.

Not someone who can only report it.

Risk Must Be Embedded in Planning – Not Reviewed Separately

In many projects, risk review happens in a separate meeting.

Planning happens elsewhere.

This separation weakens both.

Risk only matters when it changes

- Schedules
- Budgets
- Procurement timing

- Resource allocation
- Contractual positions

If the schedule does not move when a risk escalates, the system is pretending.

Strong execution cultures treat risk escalation as a planning input, not a governance ritual.

The Leadership Signal That Shapes Risk Behaviour

Teams learn very quickly what kind of risk behaviour is safe.

If leaders respond to early risk escalation with

"Why are you being negative?"

"Let us not complicate things."

"We will manage it later."

People stop escalating.

Not because risks disappear.

Because safety disappears.

In contrast, when leaders respond with

"What decision do we need to take now?"

"What flexibility do you need to reduce this risk?"

"What support do you need to act?"

Risk management becomes operational—not theoretical.

The Dangerous Narrative of "We Will Recover"

One of the most damaging beliefs in renewable execution

is the confidence in recovery.

"We are behind, but we will recover later."

This belief postpones risk action.

It converts prevention into hope.

Most projects do not fail because recovery was impossible.

They fail because recovery options disappeared while leadership waited for clarity.

Risk discipline is about acting before recovery is needed.

Closing Reflection

Risk management is not pessimism.

It is respect for complexity.

In an industry that is building increasingly interconnected, capital-intensive and time-bound infrastructure, disciplined risk ownership is no longer optional.

It is a credibility requirement.

Because in renewable execution, success is not defined by how fast we build.

It is defined by how reliably we deliver—

despite uncertainty.

Chapter – 10

EPCs, Developers & the Trust Deficit

Alignment on Paper, Mistrust on Ground.

Most renewable projects begin with optimism.

Contracts are signed. Scopes are defined. Milestones are agreed.

On paper, everyone is aligned.

On ground, mistrust quietly takes root.

This gap between contractual alignment and execution reality is where many renewable projects start to fracture.

Contracts are Not Relationships

Contracts define obligations.

They do not create trust.

In execution, trust is built through

- Transparent communication
- Predictable decisions
- Fair handling of risk

When contracts are treated as weapons instead of safeguards, collaboration collapses.

Misaligned Incentives, Predictable Behaviour

Developers often prioritize

- Timely commissioning
- Cost containment
- Investor confidence

EPCs often prioritize

- Scope clarity
- Payment certainty
- Risk limitation

When incentives are misaligned, behavior follows incentives—not intent.

Execution suffers not because parties are dishonest, but because the system rewards self-protection.

The Claim Culture Trap

Weak trust environments breed claim cultures.

Minor ambiguities become disputes. Variations become leverage. Delays become bargaining tools.

Once claims replace collaboration, execution speed drops sharply.

Risk Transfer vs. Risk Sharing

Many contracts attempt to transfer all risk to EPCs.

This looks strong on paper.

In reality, it creates defensive execution.

EPCs protect themselves instead of optimizing the project.

True execution maturity lies in risk sharing, not risk dumping.

My Learning Curve

Earlier in my career, I believed tighter contracts would guarantee performance.

They did not.

What improved outcomes was clarity, fairness, and consistent behavior.

Trust accelerated execution more than penalties ever did.

Communication Breakdowns

Mistrust distorts communication.

Information is filtered. Bad news is delayed. Decisions are escalated unnecessarily.

Execution slows—not because issues are complex, but because honesty is risky.

Building Trust without Losing Control

Trust does not mean leniency.

It means

- Clear expectations
- Consistent enforcement
- Fair treatment
- Early resolution

Strong leaders balance firmness with fairness.

The Cost of the Trust Deficit

When trust is low

- Coordination costs rise
- Legal costs increase
- Project focus shifts from delivery to defence

These costs rarely appear in budgets—but they destroy value.

Contracts Should Enable Execution

The best renewable projects treat contracts as execution frameworks, not battlegrounds.

They

- Align incentives
- Share critical risks
- Resolve disputes early
- Protect long-term relationships

Trust is a Leadership Asset

Trust cannot be delegated to contracts.

It is built—or broken—by leadership behaviour.

Even the best technology, land, evacuation, and governance cannot compensate for a trust deficit.

Because execution is a human endeavour.

The next chapter will examine how time—often underestimated—becomes the most expensive resource of all.

The First Breakdown is Always Small

Trust between a developer and an EPC rarely collapses because of one large dispute.

It collapses because of many small moments.

- A payment delayed without explanation.
- A drawing revision issued without consultation.
- A site instruction given verbally and later denied.
- A minor variation rejected on technical wording rather than intent.

Individually, these seem operational.

Collectively, they rewrite the relationship.

Once partners start protecting position instead of protecting progress, execution speed declines immediately.

The Difference Between Commercial Discipline and Commercial Aggression

Strong developers enforce contracts.

Weak developers weaponize them.

There is an important distinction.

Commercial discipline protects project viability.

Commercial aggression protects short-term leverage.

In aggressive environments, every discussion is filtered through liability.

Instead of asking,
"What is the fastest way to solve this?"

Teams ask,
"Who will be blamed if this fails?"

Execution slows not because problems are hard—but because decisions become legally fragile.

Why EPCs Stop Sharing Ideas

In low-trust projects, EPC teams quickly learn that initiative is dangerous.

If they propose a better sequencing method and it later fails, it becomes their responsibility.

If they highlight a design weakness early, it becomes a contractual admission.

So EPCs retreat into strict scope execution.

They stop contributing execution intelligence.

This is one of the most expensive losses in renewable projects.

Because EPCs often see constructability risks before anyone else does.

Trust unlocks execution intelligence.

Contracts alone do not.

The Hidden Cost of Payment Friction

Nothing damages trust faster than unpredictable payments.

Even financially strong developers unintentionally create execution drag when

- Certification cycles are slow
- Deductions are unexplained
- Approvals move through unclear channels

From the EPC's perspective, cash flow is survival.

When payment becomes uncertain, everything else becomes defensive

- Mobilisation slows
- Subcontractors are protected first
- Risk appetite collapses

Execution speed is directly linked to commercial confidence.

This is not soft behaviour.

It is rational behaviour.

Risk Sharing Must Be Visible, Not Clausal

Many contracts contain risk-sharing language.

Very few projects demonstrate it in action.

Real risk sharing shows up when

- Scope growth is acknowledged early and priced fairly
- Interface failures are jointly resolved instead of disputed
- Schedule impact is analysed collaboratively
- Recovery plans are co-owned

When leaders step in only to enforce clauses and not to resolve shared problems, trust erodes rapidly—regardless of what the contract says.

Why Early Conflict Resolution is a Leadership Responsibility

Most EPC-developer conflicts begin at site level.

If they are not resolved quickly and fairly, they climb the organisation ladder.

By the time leadership intervenes, positions are already hardened.

Execution-mature organisations intervene early—not legally, but operationally.

They ask:

"What must be clarified today to avoid a dispute tomorrow?"

Conflict prevention is far cheaper than claim settlement.

Trust is Built through Predictability

EPCs and developers do not need generosity.

They need predictability.

- Predictable decisions.
- Predictable payment behaviour.
- Predictable response to bad news.
- Predictable escalation paths.

When partners can predict how leadership will react, they can take execution risks safely.

When leadership reactions are inconsistent, people protect themselves.

The Long-Term Cost Nobody Calculates

A trust deficit does not end with one project.

It shapes future pricing, future contractor interest and future execution capacity.

Good EPCs quietly avoid developers who are commercially aggressive but operationally rigid.

The developer may still attract bidders.

But not the best ones.

Trust, over time, becomes a market filter.

Closing Reflection

Contracts create boundaries.

Trust creates momentum.

Renewable execution today is too complex, too fast and too interdependent to be delivered through contractual defense alone.

Leadership must therefore move beyond the comfort of clauses and penalties.

They must actively design collaborative execution behaviour—without compromising commercial discipline.

Because the real question is not:

"Who is contractually right?"

It is:

"Who will help this project succeed—when the contract is no longer enough?"

Chapter - 11

Policy is not the Problem

The Convenient Scapegoat

When renewable projects struggle, the first explanation offered is often policy.

Regulations changed. Approvals took time. Guidelines were unclear.

Policy becomes the convenient scapegoat for execution failure.

Yet, across India, renewable capacity continues to scale year after year—under the same policies.

If policy were truly the problem, progress would have stalled long ago.

Policy Sets Direction. Execution Determines Outcomes.

Policy provides intent.

It signals priorities, incentives, and boundaries.

Execution determines whether intent turns into commissioned assets.

Blaming policy often masks a deeper issue: lack of execution preparedness.

The Difference between Uncertainty and Unpreparedness

Policies evolve. That is expected.

Execution-mature organizations plan for change.

Execution-weak organizations are surprised by it.

The same policy environment produces radically different outcomes for different developers.

The difference is not access.

It is preparedness.

What Policy Actually Demands

Most renewable policies assume

- Timely land availability
- Evacuation coordination
- Financial closure discipline
- Compliance capability

When projects fail to meet these assumptions, policy is blamed—unfairly.

My Reality Check

I have reviewed projects delayed under the banner of policy challenges.

In most cases, the real issues were familiar

- Land not fully secured
- Evacuation not contractually aligned
- Approvals followed reactively, not proactively

Policy did not stop execution.

Preparation did.

Execution Maturity Absorbs Policy Change

Well-governed projects absorb policy changes without crisis.

They

- Track regulatory developments early
- Build buffer into timelines

- Maintain compliance readiness

Poorly governed projects experience the same changes as shocks.

Policy Literacy is an Execution Skill

Understanding policy is not the job of consultants alone.

Project leaders must

- Interpret implications
- Plan scenarios
- Align execution strategies

Policy ignorance at the execution level creates avoidable delays.

When Policy Really Hurts

Policy becomes painful only when execution is fragile.

Weak foundations amplify regulatory friction.

Strong foundations neutralize it.

Stop Outsourcing Responsibility

Blaming policy externalizes responsibility.

Execution excellence internalizes it.

Leaders who wait for perfect policy will wait forever.

The Leadership Shift Required

The question leaders must ask is not

> *"What is wrong with policy?"*

But

> *"are we prepared to execute within it?"*

This shift changes outcomes.

Policy Enables. Preparedness Delivers

India's renewable policies are directional, not operational.

They reward those who execute reliably.

Projects fail not because policy is flawed—but because execution is weak.

The next chapter will examine the most underestimated execution variable of all: ***time.***

Policy is a Constraint, Not an Excuse

Every serious infrastructure industry operates under regulatory constraints.

Aviation does.

Telecom does.

Oil and gas does.

Urban infrastructure does.

Renewable energy is not unique.

What is unique in renewables is how quickly execution teams convert regulatory complexity into an external justification for internal gaps.

Policy does not exist to make execution comfortable.

It exists to protect public interest, system stability and long-term national priorities.

Execution leadership must therefore treat policy as a design boundary—not a post-hoc explanation.

The Real Problem: Policy is Read Late

In many projects, policy is understood only when approvals are required.

By then, options are limited.

Execution-mature organizations read policy at the planning stage—not at the compliance stage.

They ask early

- What approvals will this configuration trigger?
- Which agencies will be involved?
- What sequencing constraints does the regulation introduce?

- What documentation readiness is required before site mobilisation?
- When policy is interpreted early, execution planning becomes realistic.
- When policy is discovered late, execution becomes defensive.

Why Consultants Cannot Replace Policy Ownership

Consultants and advisors play an important role in regulatory interpretation.

But execution ownership cannot be outsourced.

When project teams rely entirely on external advisors to manage regulatory interfaces, three gaps emerge

- Internal understanding remains shallow
- Regulatory timelines are assumed, not owned
- Learning is not institutionalised

Policy literacy must sit inside the execution organisation.

Otherwise, every project repeats the same mistakes.

Policy Favourably Rewards Predictability

One uncomfortable truth for many developers is this:

Regulatory authorities respond faster to predictable organisations.

Not to influential ones.

Not to aggressive ones.

To predictable ones.

Predictable submissions.

Predictable follow-ups.

Predictable compliance quality.

Predictable engagement behaviour.

Execution discipline earns regulatory credibility over time.

That credibility quietly accelerates future projects far more than escalation or lobbying ever can.

The Invisible Interface: Policy and Schedule Design

Most project schedules treat approvals as tasks.

"Apply – 30 days."

This is dangerously simplistic.

Regulatory processes are not activities.

They are workflows involving review cycles, clarifications, site inspections and internal authority movements.

Execution-mature projects therefore design schedules that reflect

- Possible clarification loops
- Document re-submission cycles
- Inspection dependencies
- Authority availability windows

Policy awareness must shape schedule logic—not be added as a line item.

Leaders Create the Policy Culture

How leadership speaks about policy determines how teams engage with it.

If policy is spoken about as an obstacle, teams treat it as something to bypass.

If policy is spoken about as an execution boundary, teams design around it.

This cultural signal matters.

In organisations where leadership routinely blames policy, people stop investing in compliance readiness.

In organisations where leadership respects regulatory realities, people build capability.

The Most Dangerous Phrase

One phrase appears repeatedly in delayed projects

"We are waiting for approval."

Waiting is not a strategy.

Behind every waiting status is usually

- An incomplete submission
- An unanswered clarification
- A missing site input
- An untracked internal workflow

Execution leadership must replace "waiting" with "what is pending, and who owns it?"

Closing Reflection

India's renewable transition is being built inside a living regulatory framework.

That framework will evolve.

That is not a weakness.

It is a sign of a maturing sector.

The real execution challenge is not policy change.

It is organisational readiness for policy reality.

Policy sets the rules of the field.

Execution determines whether your team knows how to play on it.

And in the renewable sector's next phase—where projects will be larger, more visible and more interconnected—the winners will not be those who complain best about policy.

They will be those who design their execution systems to operate confidently within it.

Chapter - 12

Time - The Most Expensive Resource

Time Does Not Appear in BOQs—But It Destroys Them

In renewable energy projects, time is rarely budgeted with honesty.

Costs are itemized. Quantities are measured. Rates are negotiated.

Time is assumed.

And yet, time is the most expensive resource a project consumes.

Every delayed day quietly compounds financial stress, operational risk, and leadership credibility.

The Compounding Effect of Delay

Delays do not add cost linearly.

They compound it.

A few weeks of slippage trigger

- Extended overheads
- Interest during construction
- Contractor claims
- Resource remobilization
- Opportunity cost of lost generation

By the time delay is visible, recovery costs exceed prevention costs many times over.

Revenue Lost is Revenue Gone Forever

Unlike manufacturing, renewable energy cannot "catch up" lost production.

A missed wind season cannot be replayed. A delayed solar commissioning cannot recover irradiance.

Lost generation is permanent loss.

No efficiency improvement later can reclaim it.

Time vs Tariff Reality

Many projects obsess over tariffs while ignoring time discipline.

A marginal tariff gain can be erased by a few months of delay.

In execution reality

Speed with certainty beats low tariff with delay.

Credibility is Time-Sensitive

Schedules are promises.

Every missed milestone weakens credibility — with: Lenders - Utilities - EPC partners - Internal teams.

Once credibility erodes, execution friction increases.

Trust slows. Decisions harden. Oversight intensifies.

Time lost early multiplies resistance later.

The Human Cost of Delay

Delays are not just financial events.

They exhaust teams.

Extended uncertainty creates: Fatigue - Attrition - Decision paralysis

Morale erodes faster than schedules.

Why Leaders Underestimate Time

Time feels abstract.

Costs feel concrete.

Leaders approve budgets with precision—but approve timelines with optimism.

Optimism is not a strategy.

My Hard Measurement

Across projects I have reviewed, one pattern is consistent

Projects delayed early almost never recover fully.

They may complete.

They rarely deliver original value.

Time Discipline is Execution Discipline

Execution-mature organizations treat time as a managed asset.

They

- Protect critical-path activities
- Build buffers consciously
- Stop non-ready parallel work
- Escalate time risk early

They measure progress by time certainty, not activity volume.

Delay is a Leadership Choice

Delays are often presented as unavoidable.

They rarely are.

Most delays originate from

- Weak readiness decisions
- Tolerance for slippage
- Late escalation

Leadership tolerance defines time outcomes.

Time Decides Winners

In renewable energy, technology parity is rising.

Execution speed and reliability will separate leaders from laggards.

Those who respect time will win capacity, capital, and credibility.

Those who don't will pay quietly—project by project.

The next chapter will focus on how organizations institutionalize speed without chaos: Building an

Execution-First Culture.

The Most Dangerous Delay is the First One

In almost every delayed renewable project I have reviewed, the most damaging delay was not the largest delay.

It was the first accepted delay.

The first time a milestone quietly slipped without consequence.

The first time a recovery plan was postponed.

The first time leadership said, "We will catch up later."

That moment resets the execution standard.

Once the organisation learns that small slippages are tolerated, time discipline collapses gradually—not dramatically.

Execution cultures do not lose control suddenly.

They lose it incrementally.

Schedule Recovery is harder than Leaders Expect

Recovery plans look attractive on paper.

Additional manpower.

Parallel fronts.

Extended shifts.

Compressed activities.

But time lost due to missing readiness cannot be recovered through acceleration.

Land access does not improve with overtime.

Evacuation approvals do not arrive faster with night shifts.

Design clarity does not improve with more people working on unstable inputs.

Execution leaders must distinguish between

Productivity delays – which can sometimes be recovered, and dependency delays – which almost never can.

Most renewable delays fall into the second category.

Time Risk Lives in Interfaces, Not Activities

Project schedules usually track activities.

But time risk accumulates at interfaces.

Between land and EPC mobilisation.

Between design freeze and procurement release.

Between evacuation readiness and commissioning.

Between payments and site productivity.

When these interfaces are misaligned, activities may appear to progress—but time is being lost silently.

This is why projects often look "on track" until suddenly they are not.

Execution-mature teams track interface readiness, not only task completion.

Why Progress Percentages Hide Time Damage

A project that is 70% complete and three months late is not 70% healthy.

Progress percentages hide two realities

- Where the remaining work sits on the critical path
- How much uncertainty still surrounds the remaining work

Time damage is not reflected in activity volume.

It is reflected in how much flexibility remains.

And flexibility is what disappears first in delayed projects.

The Leadership Habit That Protects Time

One habit separates organisations that protect time from those that lose it.

They ask a different question in reviews.

Instead of asking

"How much work did we complete this week?"

They ask

"What work on the critical path is now more certain than last week?"

Certainty—not activity—is what protects schedules.

The Silent Trade-Off Nobody Admits

Under time pressure, teams quietly trade quality and preparedness for movement.

Incomplete drawings are released.

Temporary access is accepted.

Interim arrangements are treated as final solutions.

These shortcuts often create hidden rework later.

Time saved today is paid back with interest tomorrow.

Execution maturity is the ability to refuse short-term time gains that create long-term time losses.

Time is the Only Resource You Cannot Refinance

Cost overruns can be refinanced.

Contracts can be renegotiated.

Scopes can be revised.

Lost time cannot.

In infrastructure projects, time is the only irreversible variable.

Once a season passes, once a tariff window closes, once a grid slot is missed—no amount of financial engineering can restore it.

This is why treating time casually is one of the most expensive leadership mistakes in renewable execution.

Closing Reflection

Time discipline is not about rushing.

It is about protecting readiness.

It is about enforcing sequence.

It is about refusing optimism when evidence demands realism.

The renewable sector will continue to grow.

Project sizes will increase. Interfaces will multiply.

Execution environments will become more complex.

In that future, the organisations that survive will not be those with the lowest tariffs or the fastest announcements.

They will be the ones who treat time as a governed asset—not a hopeful assumption. Because in renewable execution, time is not just money.

Time is value.

Chapter - 13

Building an Execution-First Culture

From Knowing What Fails to Designing What Works

Up to this point, this book has diagnosed failure.

Technology myths. Execution gaps. Land, evacuation, governance, people, urgency, risk, trust, policy, and time.

Diagnosis, however, does not deliver projects.

Culture does.

An execution-first culture is what converts insight into consistent outcomes.

Culture is Not Values on the Wall

Many organizations proudly display values: Integrity - Excellence - Speed - Teamwork

Yet projects still drift.

That is because culture is not what is written.

Culture is what is tolerated.

If missed milestones are tolerated, delay becomes culture. If weak ownership is tolerated, diffusion becomes culture. If firefighting is rewarded, chaos becomes culture.

The Core Principles of Execution-First Culture

Execution-first organizations are built on a few non-negotiable principles

1. Ownership before activity
2. Readiness before speed
3. Discipline before heroics
4. Clarity before urgency
5. Closure before reporting

These principles sound simple.

They are difficult to enforce.

Leadership Behaviour is the Blueprint

Culture does not cascade through emails.

It cascades through leadership behaviour.

What leaders

- Ask repeatedly
- Escalate immediately
- Ignore consistently

Becomes culture.

Execution-first leaders obsess less over presentations—and more over decisions.

Institutionalizing Ownership

Ownership cannot depend on personalities.

It must be institutional.

Execution-first organizations

- Assign single
- Point ownership for outcomes

- Define authority along with responsibility
- Protect owners when decisions are made in good faith

Without protection, ownership retreats.

Speed without Panic

Execution-first culture values speed—but not chaos.

Speed is achieved through

- Early readiness
- Clear sequencing
- Stable decision rights

Urgency is applied selectively, not emotionally.

Calm becomes a system, not a personality trait.

Systems That Reinforce Culture

Culture must be reinforced by systems.

Execution-first systems include

- Readiness gates before commitments
- Escalation matrices with time limits
- Risk ownership dashboards
- Closure-based performance reviews

Systems make discipline repeatable.

Reward What You Want Repeated.

Organizations get what they reward.

If they reward

- Firefighting → chaos multiplies
- Reporting → drift continues
- Speed alone → quality collapses

Execution-first cultures reward

- Early problem identification
- Closure under uncertainty
- Team success over individual heroics

My Cultural Reset

At one point, I realized that no new process would fix recurring execution issues.

What was needed was a cultural reset.

We stopped celebrating effort.

We started celebrating closure.

Execution improved—not overnight, but permanently.

Culture is Built One Decision at a Time

There is no workshop that creates execution-first culture.

It is built through

- Hundreds of consistent decisions
- Thousands of small reinforcements
- Zero tolerance for chronic indiscipline

Culture compounds—just like delay.

The Execution Advantage

In a sector where technology is converging and capital is available, execution culture becomes the only sustainable advantage.

Organizations that build it

- Deliver faster
- Attract better partners
- Retain stronger talent
- Earn investor confidence

Execution-first culture is not optional.

It is decisive.

Culture is Built at the Moment of Tension

Culture is not created when projects are comfortable.

It is created when something goes wrong.

- When a deadline is missed.

When a contractor fails.

When a leader is embarrassed in front of stakeholders.

When pressure arrives from the board or the lender.

At that moment, leaders choose between two responses:

protect the system

or protect the narrative.

Execution-first culture is built when leaders protect the system—even when the narrative becomes uncomfortable.

The Most Powerful Cultural Signal: Who Gets Protected

Teams watch carefully:

Who is protected when a difficult decision backfires?

Who is exposed when an assumption fails?

Who is publicly questioned—and who is privately supported?

In execution-first cultures, leaders protect people who take ownership in good faith.

Not people who avoid risk.

This single behaviour decides whether ownership grows—or disappears.

Culture is Lost Faster than it is Built

One inconsistent leadership decision can undo months of cultural reinforcement.

For example

You say readiness matters.

But you still push mobilisation without access.

You say ownership matters.

But you override a project owner publicly.

You say closure matters.

But you reward the best presentation.

People do not remember what leaders say.

They remember what leaders tolerate under pressure.

Execution Culture Must Be Designed Into Reviews

Most project reviews still revolve around activity.

Percent complete.

Milestones achieved.

Issues listed.

Execution-first reviews ask different questions

- What critical decision is pending?
- Which interface is most fragile right now?
- Which risk has no owner with authority?
- What readiness assumption are we carrying into next week?

When leadership repeatedly asks these questions, culture shifts quietly.

People prepare differently.

They think differently.

They escalate differently.

Cultural Discipline Requires Leadership Patience

Execution-first culture does not show dramatic early wins.

In fact, it can feel slower at first.

Because

More assumptions are challenged,

More readiness gates delay commitments,

More uncomfortable conversations surface early.

But over time, chaos reduces.

Recovery plans reduce.

Heroics reduce.

What increases is predictability.

Execution maturity trades excitement for reliability.

That is a difficult cultural trade-off for fast-growing organisations.

Why Middle Managers Decide the Culture

Senior leaders declare culture.

Middle managers deliver it.

If functional heads continue to reward speed over sequence,

If project managers are still judged on activity volume,

If site leaders are still praised for "managing somehow,"

Execution culture will not change—regardless of leadership intent.

Execution-first transformation must therefore focus heavily on:

Project heads,

Functional managers,

Interface leaders.

They translate philosophy into daily behavior.

Culture Requires Consequences, Not Only Communication

Most cultural change programs fail because they avoid consequences.

Execution-first culture demands visible consequences for:

Repeated readiness violations,

Chronic decision avoidance,

Unowned risks,

Silent slippage.

Not punishment.

But clarity.

When people see that indiscipline has no impact, discipline becomes optional.

The Final Cultural Test

There is a simple test to know whether execution-first culture exists.

Ask one question inside the organisation

"Who will stop this if readiness is weak?"

If the answer is unclear—or political—culture is still fragile.

In strong execution cultures, everyone knows who can stop work.

And everyone knows that stopping work to protect readiness is respected.

Closing Reflection

Execution-first culture is not motivational.

It is operational.

It does not make people work harder.

It makes people work responsibly.

In the renewable sector's next phase, where scale, scrutiny and capital discipline will increase simultaneously, culture will become a strategic differentiator—not a soft concept.

Projects will not fail because people are unwilling.

They will fail because organisations did not design behaviour that protects execution.

Execution-first culture is therefore not a leadership slogan.

It is a leadership system.

The next chapter will redefine leadership itself in this context: The Project Manager as the Real Energy Leader.

Chapter - 14

The Project Manager as the Real Energy Leader

Leadership Happens Where Execution Happens

In the renewable energy sector, leadership is often associated with boardrooms, policies, and announcements.

But energy transition does not happen in presentations.

It happens on sites.

It happens where land meets engineering, where grid meets generation, and where plans meet reality.

At that intersection stands the Project Manager.

Beyond Schedules and Checklists

For years, project managers have been viewed as execution managers—task trackers, schedule followers, issue escalators.

This view is outdated.

Modern renewable projects demand far more.

Project managers today must

- Balance technical, commercial, social, and regulatory forces
- Take decisions under ambiguity

- Lead without formal authority
- Translate strategy into reality

This is not management.

This is leadership.

Why Project Managers Shape Outcomes More than Strategy

Strategies succeed or fail based on how they are executed.

Policies materialize only when projects are delivered.

Capital creates value only when assets are commissioned.

In all three, the project manager is the decisive factor.

A strong project leader can stabilize a weak strategy.

A weak project leader can destroy a strong one.

The Energy Transition Needs Execution Leaders

India's energy transition is ambitious.

Gigawatts must be built across diverse geographies, communities, and grids. This complexity cannot be managed centrally.

It requires distributed leadership—leaders embedded within projects, empowered to decide and accountable to deliver.

Project managers are uniquely positioned to play this role.

The Leadership Gap

Many organizations still under-invest in project leadership.

They

- Overload project managers with reporting
- Under-empower them in decision-making
- Hold them accountable without authority

This gap creates frustration—and execution failure.

Redefining the Project Manager's Mandate

Execution-first organizations redefine the role clearly.

The project manager is

- The single-point owner of delivery
- The integrator of all functions
- The custodian of time, cost, and credibility
- The voice of ground reality to leadership

This clarity transforms performance.

My Shift in Perspective

Earlier in my leadership journey, I viewed project managers as operational executors. Experience changed that view.

I have seen projects rescued—not by new technology or new contracts—but by strong project leaders who restored discipline, clarity, and trust.

Energy leadership, I learned, is often exercised far from the boardroom.

Skills That Define the New Energy Leader

The modern project leader must combine

- Technical understanding
- Commercial awareness
- Stakeholder empathy
- Decision courage
- Communication clarity

This blend is rare—but essential.

Empowerment is Not Optional

Expecting leadership without empowerment is unfair.

Execution-first organizations

- Delegate authority explicitly
- Support decisions made in good faith

- Protect project leaders from political pressure

Empowered leaders deliver empowered execution.

From Project Delivery to Industry Impact

When project managers lead effectively

- Projects deliver on time
- Investors gain confidence
- Communities experience trust
- Policy intent becomes reality

In this way, project leaders do more than deliver projects.

They advance the energy transition itself.

The Quiet Leaders of the Transition

The future of renewable energy will not be shaped only by visionaries and policymakers.

It will be shaped by disciplined, courageous project leaders who deliver repeatedly under real-world constraints.

Recognizing and developing these leaders is no longer optional.

It is strategic.

The final chapter will bring this journey together—looking ahead to how execution excellence will define the winners of the renewable future.

The Project Manager as the System Integrator

The most misunderstood part of the modern project manager's role is not scheduling.

It is integration.

Renewable projects today are not technical systems alone.

They are social systems, regulatory systems, financial systems and contractual systems operating simultaneously.

The project manager is the only role that sees all of them at once.

Engineering sees design.

Finance sees cash.

Legal sees clauses.

Land teams see negotiations.

EPCs see scope.

Only the project leader sees the collision.

Leadership begins when someone owns that collision.

The Courage to Stop Work

One of the strongest indicators of real leadership is not how fast a project moves.

It is whether the project leader can stop it.

Stopping mobilisation because land access is not real.

Stopping procurement because drawings are unstable.

Stopping parallel work because interfaces are unresolved.

These decisions are deeply uncomfortable.

They create visible slowdown.

They invite scrutiny.

They create pressure from multiple directions.

But execution leaders understand a difficult truth:

If the project manager cannot stop work, they do not truly own delivery.

They only supervise activity.

Leading without Authority is a Daily Reality

Most project managers operate in environments where

- Functional teams report elsewhere
- Contractors are commercially protected
- Utilities and authorities are external

- Internal priorities compete constantly

Formal authority is limited.

Influence is everything.

This is why communication skill alone is insufficient.

Execution leadership requires

- The ability to align incentives,
- The ability to frame risk in business language,
- The ability to escalate without blame,
- The ability to hold peers accountable without hierarchy.

This is leadership under constraint.

And it is far more demanding than line management.

The Three Conversations a Real Project Leader Owns

In high-performing projects, the project manager consistently drives three conversations.

Not reports.

Conversations.

First: the readiness conversation

"What must be true before this activity starts?"

Second: the risk conversation

"What will break if we proceed now?"

Third: the decision conversation

"What choice must we make this week to protect flow?"

When these conversations disappear, execution degrades silently.

Why Great Project Leaders are Uncomfortable People

Strong execution leaders are rarely popular.

They challenge optimism.

They interrupt momentum.

They expose fragile assumptions.

They push back on senior pressure.

They escalate early.

In organizations addicted to urgency and optics, this behavior is often misunderstood.

But uncomfortable leadership protects outcomes.

Comfortable leadership protects narratives.

The energy transition needs the first.

Not the second.

Translating Strategy into Field Reality

Strategy talks about gigawatts, returns and national targets.

The project manager translates that ambition into

- Land access sequences,
- Construction fronts,
- Grid synchronization windows,
- Cash flow timing,
- Local stakeholder engagement.

This translation is not mechanical.

It is interpretive.

Every site has different constraints.

Every district behaves differently.

Every utility interface has its own rhythm.

Execution leadership is localised leadership.

And this is precisely why project managers shape outcomes more than corporate strategy teams ever can.

The Emotional Load of Project Leadership

Project leaders carry pressure that is rarely acknowledged.

They absorb

- Conflicting instructions,
- Contractor frustration,
- Site-level conflict,
- Leadership impatience,
- Public accountability.

They stand between field reality and executive expectation.

This emotional load matters.

Organizations that fail to support project leaders psychologically eventually lose their strongest execution capability.

Burnout does not show up in dashboards.

It shows up in hesitation, over-escalation and loss of judgment.

Execution maturity must therefore include leadership care—not only leadership control.

The Most Important Skill: Business Judgment

Technical competence is essential.

But it is not sufficient.

The defining capability of an execution leader is business judgment.

Knowing when to

- Accept additional cost to protect time,
- Delay mobilisation to protect quality,
- Confront a partner to protect trust,
- Escalate to protect credibility.

These decisions cannot be automated.

They require

Context,

Experience,

And courage.

This is why the project manager is not merely delivering scope.

They are protecting value.

Why Organizations Must Redesign the Project Manager Role

If project managers are expected to be real energy leaders, organizations must stop designing the role as an administrative hub.

They must

- Give project leaders direct access to decision forums,
- Delegate approval authority within defined limits,
- Formally empower them on land, evacuation and interface decisions,
- Evaluate them on outcomes—not activity metrics.

Without this structural redesign, leadership expectations remain rhetorical.

The Leadership Development India's Renewable Sector Needs

India's renewable scale-up will not be constrained by technology.

It will be constrained by leadership bandwidth.

The sector urgently needs a deliberate project leadership pipeline.

Not just engineers promoted upward.

But professionals trained in

- Interface leadership,
- Commercial negotiation,
- Regulatory engagement,
- Risk-based decision making,

- And organizational influence.

Execution excellence must become a career discipline—not an accidental outcome.

The Real Legacy of a Project Leader

A project leader's legacy is not only a commissioned plant.

It is

A trained site team,

A disciplined contractor ecosystem,

A repeatable delivery system,

And a strengthened organizational culture.

Plants depreciate.

Execution capability compounds.

This is the real contribution of great project leaders to the energy transition.

Closing Reflection

If India is serious about delivering its renewable ambition at scale, it must stop treating project managers as support roles.

They are not.

They are the operational leaders of the transition.

They carry the weight of strategy on their daily decisions.

They absorb complexity that no central function can manage.

They protect value under pressure. And in the end, when turbines turn and substations energize, it is not policy that stands on site.

It is leadership.

Project leadership.

Chapter - 15

Winning the Energy Transition

The Transition Will Be Decided on the Ground.

The renewable energy transition is often described in grand numbers—gigawatts, targets, timelines, investments.

But transitions are not won in announcements.

They are won on the ground—project by project, decision by decision, day by day.

What separates winners from laggards in the next decade will not be access to technology or capital.

It will be execution reliability.

From Ambition to Repeatability

Ambition is abundant in the renewable sector.

What is scarce is repeatable delivery.

Winning organizations are not those that deliver one exceptional project.

They are those that deliver consistently—across locations, partners, policies, and cycles.

Repeatability is a leadership outcome.

The New Competitive Advantage

As technology converges and tariffs compress, competitive advantage shifts.

It moves from

- Equipment → Execution
- Speed → Reliability
- Announcements → Commissioned assets

Execution excellence becomes strategy.

What the Winners Do Differently

Organizations that will lead the next decade share common traits

They design projects for execution, not optimism.

They institutionalize ownership and decision rights.

They treat time as a financial asset.

They manage risk proactively, not heroically.

They reward closure, not activity.

These are not slogans.

They are operating systems.

Leadership That Endures Pressure

The next phase of the energy transition will be harder, not easier.

Land will be tighter. Grids will be stressed. Communities will demand engagement. Capital will demand discipline.

Only leaders who remain calm under pressure—and disciplined under ambition—will succeed.

Trust as Infrastructure

In the coming decade, trust will be as critical as transmission lines.

Trust between

- Developers and EPCs
- Leaders and teams

- Projects and communities
- Investors and operators

Trust reduces friction.

Friction consumes time.

Time decides outcomes.

Culture Compounds Faster than Capacity

Capacity can be added quickly.

Culture cannot.

Organizations that start building execution-first culture now will compound advantage over time.

Those who delay will struggle to catch up—no matter how much capacity they announce.

The Quiet Winners

The winners of the energy transition will not always be the loudest.

They will be the most reliable.

They will deliver when others delay.

They will earn confidence when others explain.

Reliability will become reputation.

Reputation will become growth.

A Final Leadership Choice

Every organization faces a choice

Chase ambition without discipline.

Or build discipline that delivers ambition.

One creates headlines.

The other builds industries.

The Closing Truth

Technology enables the transition.

Policy directs it.

Capital accelerates it.

But execution—

Execution led by disciplined leaders and strong culture—wins it.

The future of renewable energy belongs to those who can turn intent into infrastructure, reliably and repeatedly.

That is how the energy transition will be won.

The Transition Will Not Be Won by Scale Alone

Over the next decade, renewable energy capacity in India will grow at a scale never attempted before.

But scale is not strategy.

Scale without delivery systems only increases the size of failure.

The uncomfortable reality is this

The industry has already proven that it can build projects.

What it has not yet proven—at national scale—is that it can build them predictably.

Predictability is the real frontier.

And predictability is an execution outcome.

From Project Excellence to Organizational Capability

One successful project does not make an organization strong.

It makes it lucky.

Execution leadership begins when organizations stop celebrating individual successes and start building institutional capability.

This means deliberately capturing

- What worked in land acquisition
- How evacuation risks were mitigated
- Which governance structures prevented delays
- How project leaders were supported during pressure
- How contractors were integrated into recovery planning

Winning organizations do not allow learning to remain trapped in people.

They turn experience into operating standards.

This is how reliability becomes scalable.

The Winners Will Build Fewer Projects Twice

One of the clearest execution indicators in mature organizations is how often the same mistake repeats.

Repeated land disputes.

Repeated evacuation misalignment.

Repeated interface failures.

Repeated schedule optimism.

Every repetition is a signal that learning is not institutionalized.

The winners of the energy transition will not be those who take more risk. They will be those who reduce unknowns faster than competitors.

They will systematically design out failure modes.

The Next Battle is Not Technology. It is Complexity.

The renewable sector is entering a phase where complexity, not innovation, will dominate execution.

Hybrid projects.

Storage integration.

Shared evacuation corridors.

Multiple offtake structures.

Stricter grid codes.

Deeper community engagement.

Complexity multiplies interfaces.

Interfaces multiply risk.

Risk multiplies leadership demand.

Organizations that still treat execution as an operational function will find themselves structurally unprepared.

Execution must move into the strategic core.

Leadership Must Redefine Success Metrics

Today, most leadership dashboards still prioritize

- Capacity added
- Projects launched
- Financial closure achieved

These metrics describe activity.

They do not describe reliability.

Execution-first leaders will increasingly track

- Schedule certainty at three months forward
- Number of unowned critical risks
- Interface readiness status
- Decision-cycle time for escalations
- Contractor confidence indicators
- Leadership intervention frequency

What leaders choose to measure quietly defines what the organization values.

And what organizations value is what eventually determines outcomes.

Why Talent Will Flow to Reliable Organizations

The next decade will expose a severe execution leadership shortage.

Good project leaders will become the scarcest resource in the renewable sector.

They will choose where to work based on

- Clarity of authority
- Leadership protection
- Decision maturity
- Organizational stability

Not only compensation.

Organizations that burn execution leaders through constant urgency, political interference and structural confusion will lose capability faster than they can replace it.

The winners will be those who treat execution leadership as a strategic asset—not a consumable resource.

Capital Will Follow Predictability

Investors rarely say this publicly.

But predictability matters more than ambition.

A developer that reliably commissions on time, manages risk transparently and protects asset performance becomes inherently bankable.

A developer that frequently renegotiates timelines, revises assumptions and explains delays—even with strong growth narratives—accumulates execution risk in the eyes of capital.

In the next phase of the sector, capital will quietly differentiate.

And it will reward delivery behavior—not capacity announcements.

Communities Will Judge Projects by Experience, Not Intent

As renewable infrastructure expands deeper into rural and semi-urban India, community perception will become decisive.

Not community consultation decks.

Actual experience.

Was access managed respectfully?

Were commitments honored?

Was engagement continuous or transactional?

Were issues resolved locally or escalated externally?

Execution discipline shapes social license.

Social license shapes delivery speed.

This relationship will only grow stronger.

Winning the energy transition requires operational trust—not reputational campaigns.

The Hardest Leadership Shift

The most difficult change for many leaders will be psychological.

From being seen as vision builders… to being measured as delivery system builders.

From championing targets… to defending discipline.

From celebrating starts… to insisting on finishes.

From rewarding urgency… to protecting readiness.

This shift is not glamorous.

But it is decisive.

What the Winners Will Do Differently—In Practice

They will delay projects early—so that they do not delay them later.

They will invest in land, evacuation and interface leadership as seriously as they invest in engineering.

They will build project leadership pipelines—not just technical cadres.

They will stop hiding behind policy, contractors or utilities—and instead design execution systems that absorb institutional complexity.

They will make escalation safe, not political.

They will protect owners, not narratives.

They will treat execution failures as organizational learning—not individual weakness.

And most importantly: they will refuse to scale faster than their execution capability.

The Transition is an Organizational Test

The renewable energy transition is often framed as a national challenge.

In reality, it is an organizational challenge repeated thousands of times.

Every developer.

Every EPC.

Every project team.

Every leadership group.

Each must answer the same question

Can we deliver what we promise—reliably?

Not occasionally.

Not heroically.

Reliably.

A Personal Closing Reflection

After reviewing, supporting and rescuing projects across years of renewable execution, one pattern is unmistakable.

Projects rarely fail because people do not care.

They fail because organizations do not protect execution discipline when pressure rises.

Ambition rises faster than systems.

Announcements arrive before readiness.

Targets outrun ownership.

And then leadership wonders why reality does not follow intent.

Execution excellence is not about doing more.

It is about doing what matters—at the right time, in the right order, by the right owners.

The Real Definition of Winning

Winning the energy transition does not mean becoming the largest developer.

It means becoming the most trusted one.

Trusted by

- Communities,
- Contractors,
- Utilities,
- Investors,
- And most importantly—by your own teams.

Trust is built only one way

Through consistent execution behavior.

Final Thought

India's renewable future will not be shaped by the organizations that speak best about sustainability.

It will be shaped by the organizations that can build infrastructure under uncertainty, complexity and pressure—without losing discipline.

The energy transition will be won quietly. By those who show up on site prepared.

By those who protect readiness when urgency is tempting.

By those who design systems that allow people to own outcomes.

By those who understand that execution is not the final step of strategy.

Execution is the strategy. And that is how the energy transition will truly be won.

Chapter - 16

Execution Metrics that Actually Matter

What You Measure is What You Tolerate

Every renewable energy organization claims to value execution.

Yet most continue to measure the wrong things.

Progress percentages.

Installed capacity.

Monthly billing.

Activity completion charts.

These metrics look impressive in reviews—but they rarely predict success.

Projects don't fail because activities weren't tracked.

They fail because **execution health was never measured**.

If you want different outcomes, you must measure different realities.

The Problem with Traditional Project Metrics

Traditional metrics answer comfortable questions:

How much work was planned?

How much work was reported?

How much value was billed?

They avoid uncomfortable ones

Is the project actually ready to move forward?

Are risks closing—or just being discussed?

Are dependencies resolved—or postponed?

Is the team aligned—or just busy?

As this book has shown repeatedly, projects collapse not due to lack of activity, but due to **unresolved execution friction**.

Activity metrics hide friction.

Execution metrics expose it.

From Activity Metrics to Execution Health Indicators

Execution-focused leaders track **signals**, not noise.

Below are the metrics that actually matter.

1. Readiness Index (Before Speed)

Before any major milestone, ask

Land physically available (%)

Evacuation approvals in hand (%)

Drawings frozen (%)

Contracts finalized (%)

Cash flow secured (%)

A project with 90% activity readiness but 60% dependency readiness is **not ready**.

Readiness predicts success better than schedules.

2. Risk Closure Rate (Not Risk Registers)

Most projects maintain risk registers. Few manage risks.

Track

Number of open high-impact risks

Average age of unresolved risks

Risks without named owners

Mitigation actions actually completed

A rising risk count is not the issue.

A **static risk count** is.

Unowned risks are delayed failures.

3. Decision Latency

Execution slows when decisions stall.

Measure

Average time to approve critical decisions

Number of decisions escalated but unresolved

Decisions revisited multiple times

Projects don't fail due to wrong decisions as often as they fail due to **no decisions**.

Decision speed is an execution KPI.

4. Interface Stability Score

Execution happens at interfaces

Land ↔ EPC

Engineering ↔ Site

Project ↔ Utility

Finance ↔ Execution

Track

Number of rework cycles

Scope changes post-mobilization

Handovers without readiness sign-off

Stable interfaces create flow. Broken interfaces create chaos.

5. Time Leakage Index

Time is the most expensive resource—and the least protected.

Measure

Slippage absorbed without recovery plans.

Lost seasonal generation days.

Idle manpower or equipment days.

Every "small" delay compounds.

Time once lost cannot be recovered—only explained.

6. Ownership Clarity Ratio

Ask brutally

How many critical items have a single accountable owner?

How many are "shared responsibilities"?

How many depend on goodwill rather than authority?

Shared ownership feels collaborative—but executes poorly.

Single-point ownership is not harsh. It is humane.

7. Issue Transparency Score

Healthy projects surface problems early.

Track

issues raised proactively vs. reactively.

Late surprises vs. early warnings.

Frequency of last-minute escalations.

If issues appear only at deadlines, the culture is unsafe.

Transparency is an execution multiplier.

Why Dashboards Don't Save Projects

Many organizations invest heavily in dashboards.

Dashboards don't execute.

People do.

A dashboard that reports activity without exposing friction creates false confidence. Leaders believe projects are under control—until they aren't.

Execution metrics must

Trigger conversations

Force decisions

Change behaviour

Otherwise, they are decoration.

What Execution-Mature Organizations Do Differently

Execution-mature organizations

Review readiness before approving speed.

Reward closure, not updates.

Track decision latency aggressively.

Treat time loss as value loss.

Make ownership visible and unavoidable.

They don't ask, *"How much is done?"*

They ask, *"What can still stop us?"*

A Warning to Leaders

If your metrics only make teams look good, they are lying to you.

Real execution metrics are uncomfortable.

They expose leadership gaps.

They reveal unresolved risks.

They demand decisions.

That discomfort is the price of reliability.

The Bottom Line

Execution does not fail suddenly.

It fails gradually—when early warning signs are ignored.

The right metrics don't guarantee success.

But the wrong metrics guarantee surprise.

If this book leaves you with one operational shift, let it be this:

Measure readiness, ownership, risk closure, and time—not just activity.

Because in renewable energy, **what you measure today decides what you commission tomorrow**.

The Missing Layer: Leading Indicators vs. Lagging Indicators

Most renewable projects are governed almost entirely through lagging indicators.

Installed capacity.

Monthly progress.

Billing achieved.

Manpower deployed.

These metrics describe what already happened.

Execution leaders, however, live on leading indicators.

Leading indicators tell you what is *about to fail.*

If your review system cannot predict problems at least four to eight weeks in advance, it is not an execution system. It is a reporting system.

The real power of execution metrics lies in anticipation—not explanation.

8. Constraint Exposure Index

(What is actually limiting progress right now?)

Every project, at any moment, has one or two real constraints.

Not ten.

Not a long issue list.

One or two.

Track explicitly

- Current dominant constraint (land, evacuation, drawing freeze, payment, approvals, utility interface, contractor capacity, etc.)
- How long that constraint has remained unchanged
- What decision or action would remove it

If your project review cannot answer, in one sentence:

"What is stopping this project from moving faster today?" ...then your metrics are not helping execution.

Great execution teams obsess over constraints, not tasks.

9. Readiness Drift Indicator

(Are assumptions silently becoming commitments?)

Track how many activities started under conditional readiness.

For example

- EPC mobilised before full land access
- Procurement released before drawing freeze
- Contractors appointed before payment structure finalisation
- Transmission sequencing assumed without written utility confirmation

This metric exposes organisational optimism.

A rising readiness drift is an early sign of future rework, claims and schedule collapse.

Execution-mature organisations treat conditional starts as exceptions—never as normal practice.

10. Escalation Quality Score

(Are issues being escalated for resolution—or for protection?)

Not all escalations are healthy.

Track

- Escalations with a clearly defined decision required
- Escalations with multiple unclear asks
- Escalations without recommended options
- Escalations made after deadlines vs. before deadlines

If most escalations reach leadership only when options are already lost, your organisation has a fear culture—not a performance culture.

Healthy escalation is early, specific and decision-oriented.

11. Rework Ratio

(How much of your effort is being wasted?)

Rework is one of the most expensive hidden execution killers.

Track

- Design revisions after construction started
- Civil or foundation rework
- Cable re-routing due to late interface changes
- Redo of documentation or submissions

Rework is not a technical failure.

It is a sequencing failure.

A rising rework ratio is a direct indicator of poor readiness discipline.

12. Contractor Confidence Index

(Do your partners believe you are predictable?)

This metric is rarely measured—but it matters deeply.

Through structured monthly feedback (even informal scoring), assess

- Payment predictability
- Decision clarity
- Site readiness at mobilisation

- Responsiveness of leadership
- Fairness in variation handling

Execution leaders often forget that contractor behaviour is shaped by developer behaviour.

A falling contractor confidence index predicts

- Slowing productivity
- Defensive execution
- Early claim positioning
- Poor resource allocation to your project

Trust is measurable—if leaders are willing to as

13. Leadership Intervention Frequency

(How often does the project require emergency leadership rescue?)

Track

- Number of leadership interventions required in a month
- Type of intervention (commercial, land, utility, internal alignment, conflict resolution)

High leadership intervention is not always a sign of strong leadership.

It is often a sign of weak execution systems.

As execution maturity improves, leadership involvement should shift: from firefighting → to decision enablement.

Metrics Only Work If They Change Authority

Here is the uncomfortable truth:

Most organisations fail at execution metrics not because they cannot measure them, but because the metrics do not change authority.

If a readiness score is poor—but mobilisation still proceeds,

If a risk remains unowned—but speed is still demanded,

If decision latency is high—but nobody is accountable for it,

Then metrics become theatre.

Execution metrics must have teeth.

They must trigger consequences.

Embedding Metrics into Decision Gates

Execution-mature organisations do not review metrics only in monthly dashboards.

They embed them into approval processes.

For example

Before approving EPC mobilisation

- Readiness index must be above an agreed threshold
- No open high-impact unowned risks
- Evacuation interface readiness signed off

Before approving major procurement

- Interface stability score validated
- Drawing freeze certification issued
- Rework ratio trend reviewed

Before declaring mechanical completion

- Synchronisation readiness verified
- Utility interface risk closed
- Decision backlog cleared

Metrics become entry criteria—not retrospective commentary.

Why Most KPis Fail Behaviour Change

Most KPis fail because they do not touch personal accountability.

People still get rewarded for

- Meeting activity targets
- Protecting their functional performance

- Showing "progress"

Execution metrics must directly influence

- Performance evaluations
- Promotion decisions
- Leadership credibility

If a project leader delivers fast progress with high rework, weak readiness and repeated escalations—but is still celebrated, the organisation has just taught everyone what really matters.

Metrics only shape culture when they shape careers.

A Simple Rule for Metric Design

Every execution metric must answer one of only three questions:

Are we ready?

Are we stuck?

Are we wasting time or effort?

If a metric cannot clearly answer one of these, it probably does not belong in an execution review.

Why "Green Dashboards" are Dangerous

Green dashboards create emotional comfort.

But execution does not need comfort.

It needs truth.

If your dashboards are mostly green, but

- Escalation is rising
- Leadership interventions are increasing
- Contractors are becoming defensive
- Claims are accumulating
- Commissioning keeps slipping

Then your metrics are lying.

Real execution dashboards are uncomfortable.

They expose friction.

They force alignment conversations.

They provoke leadership decisions.

India-Specific Reality: Why Execution Metrics Matter Even More

In Indian renewable execution, institutional and external dependencies are structurally higher

- District administration
- Multiple utility layers
- Land ownership fragmentation
- Row and community interfaces
- Seasonal constraints

These are not controllable risks.

They are design realities.

Execution metrics are the only way to prevent these realities from turning into late surprises.

Without early indicators, organisations discover problems only when public deadlines are missed—and reputations are already damaged.

The Cultural Shift Metrics Must Create

The real goal of execution metrics is not reporting accuracy.

It is behavioural change.

The shift you are trying to create is

From
"We are progressing."

To
"We are becoming more certain."

From

“We are busy.”

To

“Our constraints are reducing.”

From

“We are aligned.”

To

“Our decisions are closing.”

Execution health is certainty, not activity.

A Final Leadership Test

Ask your leadership team one question at your next project review

“If this project fails three months from now, which of today’s metrics would have warned us first?”

If the answer is unclear, you are still measuring outcomes — not execution health.

Closing Reflection

Great execution organisations do not wait for failure to learn.

They design metrics that make failure visible while it is still optional.

The purpose of execution metrics is not to control people.

It is to protect them from silent risk, late surprises and avoidable pressure.

In a sector where projects are getting larger, faster and more interconnected, the leaders who win will not be the ones with the most sophisticated dashboards.

They will be the ones who use the right metrics to protect readiness, force decisions, and relentlessly reduce uncertainty.

Because in renewable energy execution, you cannot manage what you cannot see, you cannot fix what you do not confront, and you cannot lead what you refuse to measure.

Chapter - 17

Stakeholders, Communities & the Social License to Execute

The Risk No Schedule Captures.

Renewable energy projects are built on land.

Land belongs to people.

Yet most project plans treat communities as a background condition—something to be "managed" after approvals are in place.

That assumption has derailed more projects than technology failures ever have.

Projects do not stall because communities are anti-development.

They stall because **execution leaders underestimate the power of social consent**.

This chapter introduces a reality many organizations learn too late:

No project executes sustainably without a social license to operate.

What is the Social License to Execute?

The social license to execute is not a legal document.

It is not a one-time agreement.

It does not come from a government office.

It is the **ongoing acceptance of a project by the people who live around it**.

When the social license exists

- Access is smoother
- Conflicts surface early
- Issues are resolved locally
- Delays reduce organically

When it does not

- Work stops without warning
- Local resistance escalates
- Administrative pressure increases
- Timelines collapse silently

Social license is not sentiment.

It is **execution risk management**.

Why Technical Projects Fail for Social Reasons

From an engineering perspective, renewable projects are predictable.

From a social perspective, they are not.

Communities experience projects very differently than developers do.

For them, a project is not

- A megawatt number
- A commissioning date
- A tariff benchmark

It is

- Land access disruption
- Livelihood uncertainty
- Construction disturbance

- Long-term presence in their geography

When this gap in perception is ignored, resistance emerges—not always loudly, but persistently.

And resistance consumes time.

Stakeholders You Cannot Afford to Ignore

Execution leaders must expand their definition of stakeholders.

Beyond investors and utilities, critical stakeholders include

- Local landowners (even after acquisition)
- Adjacent farmers and residents
- Village leadership and informal influencers
- Local contractors and workforce
- District-level administration

Ignoring informal influence while managing formal approvals is a common execution mistake.

Projects fail socially long before they fail administratively.

The Cost of Treating Communities as a Compliance Task

Many projects follow a predictable but flawed pattern:

1. Secure land legally
2. Begin construction quickly
3. Address community issues reactively
4. Escalate to administration when resistance grows

This approach creates

- Distrust
- Polarization
- Dependency on authority instead of cooperation

Administrative force may restart work temporarily—but it permanently damages trust.

Trust, once broken, does not recover on schedules.

Engagement is Not CSR. It is Execution Discipline.

Community engagement is often delegated to CSR teams or junior resources.

That is a mistake.

Engagement decisions affect

- Site access
- Work continuity
- Local workforce stability
- Long-term operational peace

These are execution outcomes.

Effective execution leaders

- Engage early, before mobilization
- Listen more than they explain
- Address small grievances before they escalate
- Ensure consistency between promises and actions

Respect creates speed. Dismissal creates delay.

Common Myths about Community Resistance

Myth 1: "People will adjust once the project starts."
Reality: Resistance hardens once people feel ignored.

Myth 2: "Legal ownership is enough."
Reality: Social acceptance matters more than paperwork.

Myth 3: "Administration will handle it."
Reality: Administration can enforce access, not cooperation.

Myth 4: "This is not the project team's job."
Reality: Anything that delays execution is the project team's job.

The Role of the Project Manager

Project managers are uniquely positioned to manage social license because they

- See issues early
- Control sequencing
- Influence contractor behavior
- Translate intent into action

A strong project manager

- Builds local rapport personally
- Ensures site teams behave respectfully
- Intervenes before escalation
- Keeps leadership informed without panic

Social risk ignored at the site level becomes a leadership crisis later.

Measuring Social Execution Health

Just as this book argues for execution metrics, social health must also be monitored.

Execution-mature organizations track

- Frequency of local disruptions
- Nature of grievances (recurring vs new)
- Time taken to resolve local issues
- Dependence on administration for access

If access requires constant authority intervention, social license is weak—even if work continues.

Long-Term Operations Begin during Construction

Social license does not end at commissioning.

Operations teams inherit the consequences of construction behavior:

Respectful projects enjoy smoother O&M

Hostile projects face recurring friction

Execution leaders who think beyond commissioning design projects for **long-term coexistence**, not short-term speed.

A Leadership Truth

Communities do not oppose renewable energy.

They oppose being ignored.

The fastest projects are not those that push hardest.

They are those that move with consent.

The Bottom Line

In renewable energy execution

- Technology builds assets
- Capital funds them
- Policy enables them

But communities decide whether they move smoothly—or not at all.

If you want reliable execution, earn the social license deliberately.

Because **projects may be approved on paper—but they are executed among people**.

The Risk No Schedule Captures—But Everyone Pays For

Social resistance rarely shows up in formal risk registers.

It appears as

- A delayed gate opening in the morning
- A blocked access road
- A contractor refusing to deploy local labour
- A sudden visit from local leaders
- An unexpected administrative inspection

These events are logged as “site issues.”

In reality, they are execution symptoms of a weak social license.

By the time social friction becomes visible in project dashboards, it has already matured into delay.

Social Risk is an Interface Risk

One of the most important reframing execution leaders must make is this:

Community risk is not a soft issue.

It is an interface risk.

It sits at the interface between

- Land and construction
- Contractors and local labour
- Administration and execution
- Long-term operations and short-term delivery

Just like technical interfaces, social interfaces must be owned.

When no one owns them, friction accumulates silently.

Why Early Mobilisation without Social Readiness is Dangerous

Projects often accelerate mobilisation immediately after land closure.

From an execution standpoint, this looks efficient.

From a community standpoint, it feels sudden and imposed.

Heavy equipment arrives.

Boundaries change.

Noise begins.

Access routes shift.

When these changes occur before social alignment, communities interpret speed as disregard.

The result is predictable

Trust erodes before work even stabilises.

Execution-mature organisations therefore treat community readiness as a mobilisation gate—just like land access or drawing freeze.

The Contractor Multiplier Effect

Most social interactions during construction are not handled by the developer.

They are handled by contractors.

Contractor supervisors.

Security staff.

Transport operators.

Subcontractors.

These people become the daily face of the project.

Execution leaders often underestimate how quickly one disrespectful incident can undo months of engagement.

Common failure patterns include

- Aggressive behaviour by security staff
- Unauthorised use of village roads
- Damage to irrigation channels or field boundaries
- Hiring practices that exclude locals

None of these appear in EPC contracts.

But all of them shape execution reality.

A project leader who does not actively govern contractor behaviour on social conduct is indirectly accepting social risk.

Community Expectations are Not Static

A dangerous assumption in renewable projects is

"We addressed community issues during land acquisition."

Community expectations evolve.

Before construction

People worry about land, compensation and access.

During construction

They worry about disturbance, jobs, safety and fairness.

During operations

They worry about permanence, benefits and unresolved grievances.

Execution leadership must therefore treat community engagement as a life-cycle activity—not a pre-construction formality.

The Hidden Stakeholder: Women and Elder Community Members

In many rural contexts, engagement is conducted primarily with male landowners or formal village representatives.

This is operationally convenient.

But it is socially incomplete.

Women and elderly community members often.

Experience project impact differently

- Water access disruption
- Safety concerns
- Livestock movement
- Noise and dust exposure

Their dissatisfaction may not surface in formal meetings.

But it influences household sentiment.

Household sentiment influences collective behaviour.

Ignoring these voices creates delayed resistance that surprises project teams later.

Why Escalation to Administration is a Strategic Failure

Administrative support is important.

But when projects rely on administration to resolve community conflict, it signals a breakdown in execution leadership.

Every time access is restored through authority rather than agreement, trust weakens.

The short-term project may move.

The long-term relationship deteriorates.

And in multi-phase developments or future projects in the same region, this cost multiplies.

Execution leaders must view administrative intervention as a last resort—not an execution tool.

Social License is Built through Predictability

Communities do not expect perfection.

They expect consistency.

They watch

- Whether commitments are honoured
- Whether the same people show up repeatedly
- Whether explanations remain stable
- Whether timelines shift without communication

Execution credibility in communities is built the same way as with lenders or contractors:

Through predictable behaviour.

Changing narratives erode trust faster than difficult truths.

The Economic Reality of Local Employment

Local employment is one of the most sensitive—and misunderstood—dimensions of social license.

Projects often promise "local jobs."

But execution reality includes

- Specialised skill requirements
- Safety certifications
- Contractor hiring systems
- Productivity pressures

When expectations and delivery diverge, resentment grows.

Execution leaders must therefore manage employment expectations explicitly.

Not through vague promises.

But through

- Transparent role definitions
- Clear duration expectations
- Fair rotation practices
- Visible grievance resolution

Ambiguity around employment becomes one of the fastest triggers for site conflict.

Designing a Social Interface Owner

Just as projects assign interface owners for evacuation, utilities or design coordination, execution-mature organisations assign a social interface owner.

This role is not ceremonial.

It must

- Maintain a live stakeholder map
- Track unresolved local issues
- Coordinate with contractors on conduct
- Advise the project leader on social readiness
- Escalate emerging risks early

Without a named owner, social risk becomes everybody's responsibility—and therefore nobody's.

Integrating Social Risk into Project Reviews

Social execution health must appear in leadership reviews.

Not as CSR updates.

As delivery risk.

Execution-mature reviews include

- Sites where access was disrupted in the past month
- Nature of grievances raised and closed
- Administrative dependency trend
- Contractor behaviour incidents
- Unresolved community commitments

If leadership never reviews social health, teams quickly learn that it is not execution-critical.

The Cultural Gap between Corporate and Local Reality

One of the most damaging mistakes execution leaders make is projecting corporate logic onto community behaviour.

Communities do not think in milestones.

They think in seasons.

They do not think in project phases.

They think in daily disruption.

They do not think in IRR.

They think in livelihood continuity.

Execution leadership requires cultural translation—not explanation.

Social License Protects More than Access

A strong social license delivers benefits beyond smoother construction.

It protects

- Theft and vandalism risk
- Sabotage risk
- Misinformation spread
- Political exploitation of local grievances

Projects with weak social license often become convenient targets during unrelated local or regional tensions.

Execution leaders must understand that social alignment is a risk buffer—not only an access facilitator.

The Leadership Presence That Matters

One of the strongest signals to communities is leadership presence.

Not inauguration visits.

Problem-solving visits.

When senior project or organisational leaders show up during local tension—and listen before instructing—community perception changes immediately.

Execution leadership is visible leadership.

Closing Reflection

The renewable sector often speaks about sustainability in terms of carbon, technology and finance.

But sustainable execution is social before it is technical.

Projects exist within communities.

Not outside them.

The real execution test is not how fast you build when everything is aligned.

It is how you behave when alignment is fragile.

Social license is not earned through communication.

It is earned through conduct.

And in the coming decade, as renewable infrastructure spreads deeper into lived landscapes, the organisations that master social execution will quietly out-deliver those that only master engineering.

Because in the real world of renewable delivery, acceptance is not optional.

It is operational.

Chapter - 18

Institutional Memory - Why Organizations Keep Repeating the Same Mistakes

Experience is Not the Same as Learning

Most renewable energy organizations proudly claim experience.

Years in operation.

Gigawatts installed.

Dozens of projects completed.

Yet the same mistakes repeat—project after project.

Land issues resurface.

Evacuation surprises return.

Governance collapses again.

Coordination breaks down in familiar ways.

The uncomfortable truth is this:

Experience does not automatically become institutional memory.

Organizations do not forget because people are careless.

They forget because **learning is not designed into execution systems**.

What Institutional Memory Really Means

Institutional memory is not a document repository.

It is not a "lessons learned" presentation.

It is not a closing workshop after commissioning.

Institutional memory exists only when

- Past mistakes actively influence present decisions
- Teams behave differently because of prior failures
- Systems prevent repetition, not just record it

If a mistake can happen again in the same way, memory has not been built.

Why Lessons Learned Rarely Change Outcomes

Most organizations conduct lessons-learned sessions.

Few change behavior afterward.

Why?

Because lessons are

- Documented after pressure has passed
- Owned by no one
- Detached from future decision-making
- Stored where execution teams never look

A lesson that does not alter approvals, checklists, or authority is not a lesson. It is commentary.

The Real Reasons Organizations Forget

1. People Move, Knowledge Leaves

Project managers rotate.

Consultants exit.

Contractors change.

When knowledge lives in people instead of systems, it disappears quietly.

2. Success is Celebrated, Failure is Buried

Organizations showcase wins.

Failures are softened, explained, or forgotten.

But unexamined success is dangerous—and unexamined failure is fatal.

3. Pressure Rewards Speed Over Reflection

The next project starts before the last one is digested.

Momentum replaces learning.

4. No One Owns Memory

Execution teams deliver.

Strategy teams plan.

No one owns *organizational learning.*

What is owned gets done.

What isn't owned gets repeated.

The Cost of Weak Institutional Memory

Weak institutional memory creates

- Repeated delays
- Increasing buffers instead of better execution
- Growing dependence on individuals
- Fragile scalability

Organizations grow in size but not in maturity.

And maturity—not scale—determines reliability.

What Execution-Mature Organizations Do Differently

Execution-mature organizations treat memory as infrastructure.

They design systems that **force learning into behavior**.

They

- Convert failures into mandatory readiness checks
- Embed past risks into approval gates
- Change authority rules based on prior breakdowns
- Update playbooks—not presentations
- Most importantly, they institutionalize discomfort.
- They do not sanitize failure.
- They operationalize it.

Turning Experience into Memory: Practical Shifts

1. Replace "Lessons Learned" with "Rules Changed"

Ask one question after every project

What rule must change so this cannot happen again?

If no rule changes, learning has failed.

2. Create Non-Negotiable Readiness Gates

If evacuation delayed once, it becomes a hard gate forever.

Memory must restrict optimism.

3. Standardize What Hurt Most

Painful experiences should become standardized checks—not optional wisdom.

4. Reward Leaders Who Surface Failure Early

Organizations remember what they reward.

If failure disclosure is punished, memory will never form.

The Role of Leadership in Memory Building

Institutional memory is a leadership responsibility.

Leaders decide

- Which failures are discussed
- Which are buried

- Which become rules

If leaders move on quickly, organizations forget quickly.

If leaders insist on structural change, organizations mature.

Institutional Memory is the Ultimate Competitive Advantage

Technology equalizes.

Capital flows.

People change.

But organizations that remember execute differently.

They

Make fewer "first-time" mistakes.

Recover faster when things go wrong.

Scale without chaos.

Earn trust repeatedly.

In the next decade, **the most reliable renewable energy companies will not be the most ambitious**.

They will be the ones that remember.

A Final Warning

If your organization says

"This happened before also…"

And nothing changes—

Then the next failure is already scheduled.

The Bottom Line

Projects fail when execution is weak.

Organizations fail when learning is weak.

Institutional memory is not about the past.

It is about protecting the future from repetition.

Build it deliberately.

Because in renewable energy execution, **forgetting is the most expensive habit of all.**

The Most Dangerous Form of Experience

The most dangerous form of experience in renewable execution is ***unquestioned familiarity.***

"We have done this many times."

This sentence appears in almost every delayed project review.

Familiarity creates comfort.

Comfort creates shortcuts.

Shortcuts create repetition.

Execution maturity is not the ability to repeat tasks faster.

It is the ability to question routines before they become liabilities.

Organizations that fail repeatedly are not inexperienced.

They are over-familiar with their own blind spots.

Institutional Memory Lives in Decisions, Not in Databases

Most organizations attempt to build memory through systems.

Knowledge portals.

Shared drives.

Project close-out folders.

Standard templates.

But execution teams do not consult folders when they are under pressure.

They consult authority.

Real institutional memory is embedded in

- Who can approve mobilisation
- Who can override readiness

- What evidence is required before commitment
- What risks block progress automatically

If past failures do not change future approval behavior, memory does not exist.

Where Repetition Actually Starts

Repetition rarely begins at site.

It begins in corporate approvals.

The same early signals appear repeatedly

- Land still being closed while EPC is mobilised
- Evacuation interfaces assumed but not contractually locked
- Drawings frozen "in principle"
- Approvals treated as timelines instead of workflows

These decisions are not made by junior teams.

They are made by leadership under ambition.

Institutional memory must therefore reshape leadership behavior—not only execution behavior.

The Two Types of Memory Organizations Confuse

Most companies confuse two very different concepts.

Project memory and Organizational memory.

Project memory ends when the project team dissolves.

Organizational memory begins only when learning survives that dissolution.

If your execution quality drops every time a strong project leader leaves, you do not have institutional memory.

You have individual excellence.

Why Post-Project Reviews Fail

Post-project reviews fail for three predictable reasons.

First, they happen when emotional distance is already high.

People are relieved.

Pressure is gone.

Attention has shifted.

Second, they are retrospective.

They ask
"What went wrong?"

They rarely ask
"What decision allowed this to happen?"

Third, they do not alter future authority.

- No gate changes.
- No approval logic changes.
- No role boundaries change.

Without structural consequence, learning evaporates.

Build Memory at the Moment of Failure—not at the End

Execution-mature organizations capture learning at the moment of friction.

When

- Land access stops work
- A utility interface blocks commissioning
- A contractor raises a major claim
- A community issue escalates
- An approval misses its expected window

The organization immediately records three things

What decision allowed this exposure?

Who had the authority to prevent it?

What rule must change from tomorrow?

Learning must be contemporaneous.

Delayed learning is diluted learning.

Failure Must Create Friction in the System

One of the strongest signals of institutional memory is *new friction.*

A painful failure should make future execution slightly harder.

Not easier.

For example

After an evacuation delay,

Generation mobilisation should require more proof—not less.

After a land dispute,

Access verification should become more intrusive—not optional.

After repeated rework,

Drawing freeze criteria should become stricter.

Memory should slow down bad decisions.

If learning makes execution faster without increasing certainty, it is probably superficial.

The Most Powerful Memory Tool: Mandatory Evidence

Execution-mature organizations shift from verbal readiness to evidential readiness.

Not

"We expect land next week."

But

"Show signed access, physical handover confirmation and site walkdown record."

Not

"Utility confirmed informally."

But

"Show written approval, approved protection scheme and testing window."

Not

"Risk is being managed."

But

"Show mitigation completed and risk closed."

Memory becomes embedded when evidence replaces optimism.

Why Digital Tools Alone Will Not Save You

Many organizations invest in digital platforms for knowledge management and project analytics.

These tools help visibility.

They do not change behavior.

Behavior changes only when

- Approvals depend on data
- Progress depends on proof
- Authority depends on compliance

Digital memory must be linked to decision rights.

Otherwise, it becomes another reporting layer.

Middle Management is the Real Memory Layer

Senior leaders create direction.

Project teams deliver.

But institutional memory is preserved—or destroyed—by middle management.

Functional heads.

Portfolio managers.

Regional leaders.

They decide whether

- Gates are enforced or bypassed
- Standards are applied or negotiated
- Exceptions become precedents

If middle management continues to trade discipline for speed, memory will collapse—no matter how strongly leadership communicates learning.

Institutional Memory Requires One Explicit Owner

This is the most overlooked design element.

Someone must own organizational learning.

Not HR.

Not quality.

Not strategy.

Execution learning.

This role must

- Track recurring failure patterns across projects
- Propose rule changes to leadership
- Update readiness gates and playbooks
- Audit whether changes are actually applied
- Intervene when standards are bypassed

Without an owner, memory remains informal.

Informal memory disappears.

The Memory Test Every Leader Should Apply

Ask this question

"If I remove my three best project leaders tomorrow, will my execution quality remain stable?"

If the honest answer is no, your organization does not yet have institutional memory.

You have talent.

Not systems.

The Cost of Over-Customization

Another hidden enemy of memory is excessive project customization.

Every project is declared "unique."

Terrain is different.

State policies are different.

Grid conditions are different.

Communities are different.

All of that is true.

But execution failures are often not unique.

They follow patterns.

If every project is treated as exceptional, no standard can survive.

Execution-mature organizations standardize the failure patterns—not the geography.

The Transition from Blame to Pattern Recognition

Weak organizations investigate failures.

Strong organizations identify patterns.

They stop asking

"Who made the mistake?"

They start asking

"In how many projects has this failure mode appeared?"

This shift transforms culture.

People stop hiding.

Leaders stop reacting.

Systems start evolving.

Institutional memory grows only in blame-safe environments.

Why Institutional Memory is a Growth Constraint

As renewable companies scale, complexity increases faster than learning.

- New regions.
- New partners.
- New grids.
- New policy environments.
- New people.

If institutional memory does not scale at the same speed, execution quality collapses silently.

This is why many fast-growing developers experience

- Rising coordination failures
- Increasing claims
- More leadership firefighting
- Lower delivery predictability

Growth exposes memory weakness.

A Closing Leadership Reality

Execution reliability is not built by adding more project controls.

It is built by removing repeatable mistakes.

And the only way to remove repeatable mistakes is to remember them structurally.

Not emotionally.

Not narratively.

Structurally.

Final Reflection

Organizations do not fail because they lack experience.

They fail because they fail to convert experience into constraint.

Real institutional memory is uncomfortable.

It slows optimism.

It questions confidence.

It blocks shortcuts.

It demands evidence.

But it also protects people.

It protects projects.

It protects leadership credibility.

In the renewable sector's next phase—where scale, speed and scrutiny will rise together—the organizations that win will not be those that learn the fastest.

They will be those that forget the least.

Chapter - 19

A Letter to Execution Leaders–Guidance for the Next Generation

This Chapter is Written for You

If you are reading this book as a project manager, engineer, or young execution professional, this chapter is written directly for you.

Not for your designation.

Not for your résumé.

But for the role you will quietly play in deciding whether the renewable energy transition succeeds or stumbles.

Throughout this book, we have examined why renewable energy projects fail—despite good technology, supportive policy, and capable organizations. The conclusion has been consistent and unavoidable:

Projects fail when execution leadership is weak.

Execution leadership does not sit only in boardrooms. It lives on sites, in meetings, during difficult phone calls, and in moments when decisions are uncomfortable but necessary.

Move Beyond the Mindset of a Coordinator

Most upcoming project managers are trained to coordinate.

To track activities.

To prepare schedules.

To escalate issues.

Coordination is necessary—but it is not sufficient.

Execution leaders think differently. They do not ask, *"is this my scope?"*

They ask, *"Will this delay my project?"*

If land is not fully available, it is your problem.

If evacuation is uncertain, it is your problem.

If payments are misaligned, it is your problem.

Ownership is not written in job descriptions.

It is claimed through behavior.

Readiness is Your First Responsibility

Every project is under pressure to move fast.

Deadlines will be announced aggressively.

Urgency will be communicated emotionally.

Shortcuts will be encouraged subtly.

Your responsibility is to slow the project down **before** it speeds up.

Ask uncomfortable questions early

- Is the land physically available—or only on paper?
- Is evacuation approved—or just verbally assured?
- Are drawings frozen—or still evolving?
- Are contractors mobilized with clarity—or confusion?

Speed without readiness does not save time.

It transfers failure into the future.

Learn to See Interfaces, Not Activities

Most project managers focus on tasks.

Execution leaders focus on interfaces.

Projects fail not because tasks are incomplete, but because handoffs are broken

- Land handed over without access
- Engineering issued without site validation
- EPC mobilized without evacuation clarity
- Payments released without readiness

Your job is to make these interfaces visible, uncomfortable, and resolved early.

Escalate Early, Not Emotionally

One of the hardest lessons for young professionals is learning **when and how** to escalate.

Late escalation is costly.

Silent escalation is destructive.

Good escalation is

- Early
- Fact-based
- Solution-oriented
- Courageous

Bad news does not damage projects.

Late bad news does.

Time is Not a Schedule. It is Value.

Treat time with the seriousness it deserves.

Every day lost

- Increases cost
- Reduces credibility
- Exhausts teams
- Destroys irreversible generation opportunity

Protect the critical path relentlessly.

Challenge unrealistic optimism respectfully.

Refuse commitments that are not ready.

Your reputation will be built on how reliably you protect time.

Build Trust without Losing Discipline

Execution accelerates in trust-rich environments.

But trust does not mean softness.

It means fairness, predictability, and consistency.

When people trust you

- They surface issues early
- They take ownership
- They collaborate instead of defend

When they fear you

- They hide problems
- They delay bad news
- They protect themselves

Choose which culture you want to create.

Develop Decision Courage

Execution leadership requires decisions under uncertainty.

Waiting for perfect information is itself a decision—and usually the wrong one.

Use judgment.

Take responsibility.

Stand by decisions made in good faith.

Indecision is more damaging than imperfect decisions.

Understand the Larger Responsibility You Carry

You may not draft policy.

You may not announce targets.

But you are the one who converts ambition into infrastructure.

Every megawatt commissioned on time builds confidence in the energy transition.

Every delayed project erodes it.

That is leadership.

A Final Message

Do not measure your success by how busy you are.

Measure it by how reliably your projects deliver.

The renewable energy sector does not need more activity.

It needs **execution leaders**.

If you internalize the discipline, ownership, and courage discussed in this book, your impact will extend far beyond any single project.

You will not just manage projects.

You will help build the future.

Learn to Say "No" Before You Learn to Say "Yes"

One of the most important professional skills you will ever develop is the ability to say *no*—early, respectfully and with evidence.

You will be asked to

- Start work before land access is real
- Mobilize contractors before drawings are frozen
- Commit dates before utilities confirm windows
- Release payments before readiness is verified

Saying yes feels cooperative.

Saying no feels risky.

But understand this clearly

- Every early yes that ignores readiness becomes a future crisis that you will be expected to solve.
- Execution leadership is not about being agreeable.

It is about being accountable.

Do Not Confuse Busyness with Value

You will be busy.

You will attend meetings.

Prepare presentations.

Answer calls late at night.

Update trackers.

Follow up endlessly.

But ask yourself one simple question every week:

What did I remove as a risk from my project this week?

If your answer is only
"I followed up."

You are managing motion—not outcomes.

The best execution leaders reduce uncertainty.

They close gaps.

They remove constraints.

Busyness is common.

Progress is rare.

Build Your Personal Execution Radar

Over time, you must train yourself to notice weak signals.

Not failures.

Signals.

Such as

- Contractors quietly slowing down mobilization
- Repeated rework requests from engineering
- Small community complaints increasing in frequency
- Payment clarifications becoming longer and defensive
- Decisions being pushed from meeting to meeting

These are not isolated issues.

They are early indicators.

Most projects fail loudly only at the end.

Strong project leaders detect failure quietly at the beginning.

Develop this radar.

It will protect your projects—and your credibility.

Learn the Language of Every Function

You cannot lead execution if you only speak engineering.

You must learn to speak

- Finance (cash flow, working capital, exposure, certification logic)
- Contracts (variation mechanisms, liability boundaries, notice timelines)
- Land and legal (possession, access, mutation, consent, encumbrance)
- Utilities and grid (testing windows, protection coordination, readiness sequence)
- Administration (process flow, authority movement, practical timelines)

You do not need to become an expert.

But you must become conversant.

Execution leadership is translation.

Between silos.

Between interests.

Between risk and action.

Protect Your Integrity Ruthlessly

You will face pressure to adjust narratives.

To soften realities.

To delay uncomfortable updates.

To "manage perception."

Short-term narrative protection always creates long-term damage.

Once you become known as someone who hides reality—even politely—your influence collapses.

Strong execution leaders earn something very rare

Credibility under pressure.

People believe them.

Leadership listens to them.

Contractors respect them.

Protect that reputation.

It is your most valuable professional asset.

Learn to Document Decisions, Not Just Minutes

One of the most underestimated execution skills is decision documentation.

Not long emails.

Not meeting notes.

Decision clarity.

Always capture

- What decision was made
- Who made it
- What assumption it depends on
- What risk was accepted
- What follow-up confirms it

When projects become complex, memory becomes unreliable.

Documentation protects

You,

Your team,

And the project.

It is not bureaucracy.

It is execution hygiene.

Understand That Leadership Will Test You Quietly

Leadership rarely tests young execution leaders through big announcements.

They test you through small moments.

They observe

- Whether you speak up when something is wrong
- Whether you remain calm when challenged
- Whether you stand by facts when pressure rises
- Whether you defend readiness even when speed is demanded

Your leadership trajectory will be shaped more by these invisible moments than by your technical output.

Do Not Wait for Authority to Start Leading

You may think

"When I become project head, I will change how things are done."

That is a trap.

Execution leadership begins long before authority arrives.

You lead when

- You frame problems clearly
- You propose solutions instead of only issues
- You connect teams that are misaligned
- You insist on clarity when confusion is convenient

If you wait for designation to start leading, you will never build leadership capability.

Learn to Manage Upward—Without Fear

One of the hardest skills for young professionals is managing upward.

Not politically.

Professionally.

It means

- Helping senior leaders understand ground reality without drama
- Protecting them from late surprises
- Giving them choices, not only problems
- Being precise, not emotional

Senior leaders do not need more information.

They need better framing.

Execution leaders become trusted when they convert complexity into decision-ready insight.

Build Relationships Before You Need Them

Do not wait for crisis to build relationships.

Spend time with

- Land teams
- Utility engineers
- District-level staff

EPC site managers subcontractor supervisors

Not for influence.

For understanding.

When pressure arrives—and it always will—projects move faster when relationships already exist.

Execution leadership is relational before it is positional.

Take Care of Yourself—This Work is Demanding

Execution leadership is intense.

Long hours.

Conflicting pressures.

Constant problem-solving.

Emotional load.

If you do not protect your own physical and mental stability, your decision quality will suffer.

Fatigue makes people

- Risk-averse
- Overly reactive
- Conflict-avoiding
- Impatient

All of which damage execution.

Sustainable leadership requires sustainable personal discipline.

This is not weakness.

It is professionalism.

Remember That You Represent More than a Project

Whether you realize it or not, you represent

Your organization,

The renewable industry,

And the idea of responsible development.

Your behavior on site becomes the face of the energy transition for local communities.

Your decisions shape contractor culture.

Your integrity shapes internal standards.

Execution leadership has reputational impact far beyond your role.

When You Fail—and You Will—Fail Well

You will make mistakes.

You will misjudge situations.

Trust the wrong signals.

Underestimate risk.

Delay escalation once or twice.

This is inevitable.

What matters is not perfection.

What matters is how you respond.

Fail well by

- Owning the mistake early
- Fixing what you can immediately
- Protecting your team from blame
- Extracting learning before moving on

Execution leaders grow fastest through honest failure.

Not hidden failure.

Build Your Own Execution Playbook

As you progress, consciously build your personal execution playbook.

Capture

- Readiness questions that saved you
- Early warning signs you missed

- Escalation patterns that worked
- Stakeholder behaviors that created risk
- Contractor practices that helped execution

Do not wait for your organization to create institutional memory.

You start by creating your own.

Great execution leaders arrive prepared—because they remember.

One Reality You Must Accept Early

You will not receive public credit for most of your good decisions.

The projects will commission.

The announcements will be made.

The leaders will speak.

The presentations will highlight success.

Your contribution will often remain invisible.

This is the nature of execution leadership.

If you seek visibility, execution will disappoint you.

If you seek outcomes, execution will reward you.

The Kind of Leader the Energy Transition Needs

The renewable energy transition does not need louder leaders.

It needs steadier ones.

It needs leaders who

- Protect readiness under pressure
- Defend truth under optimism
- Build trust under tension
- Take responsibility under ambiguity

You do not need to become famous to be influential.

You need to become reliable.

A Final Personal Note to You

One day, years from now, you will stand on a site and watch a substation energize.

Or see turbines turn for the first time.

Or watch the SCADA screen light up.

In that moment, no one will remember

- How many meetings you attended,
- How many mails you sent,
- How many trackers you maintained.

But you will remember

- The decisions you defended,
- The shortcuts you refused,
- The risks you escalated,
- The people you protected.

That is execution leadership.

And that is what will quietly shape the future of renewable energy in this country.

Closing Message

Do not become only a good project manager.

Become a reliable execution leader.

Your career will grow.

But more importantly—

The future will be built more safely, more responsibly, and more predictably because of people like you.

Chapter - 20

Why this Book Matters

Why Renewable Energy Projects Don't Fail on Technology- They Fail on Execution

The renewable energy sector is entering a decisive phase.

Technology has matured. Capital is available. Policy intent is clear. Yet across India and other emerging markets, renewable energy projects continue to suffer from delays, cost overruns, stranded assets, and eroding credibility with investors, utilities, and communities.

The common explanations—technology limitations, policy uncertainty, or external delays—are no longer convincing.

The real issue is execution.

This book matters because it addresses the **single most underexplored gap in the renewable energy transition**: the failure of execution systems, leadership behavior, and organizational culture to keep pace with ambition.

What Problem this Book Solves

Most existing books on renewable energy focus on

- Technology innovation
- Policy frameworks
- Market targets and capacity growth

Very few address **why projects fail on the ground even when all of the above are in place**.

This book directly confronts that gap by answering questions leaders quietly struggle with:

- Why do world-class projects still miss commissioning deadlines?
- Why do land and evacuation issues keep repeating despite experience?
- Why does governance collapse into firefighting under pressure?
- Why do capable teams deliver inconsistent outcomes?
- Why do contracts fail to protect execution?
- Why does time destroy value faster than cost overruns?

By reframing renewable energy success as an **execution and leadership challenge**, this book provides a missing lens for the sector.

Why this Book is Timely

The next decade of renewable energy will be fundamentally different from the last.

- Tariffs are compressing
- Grids are stressed
- Capital is becoming more selective
- Delivery certainty matters more than announcements

In this environment, **execution reliability will be the primary competitive advantage**.

Organizations that can consistently deliver projects—on time, with discipline and trust—will win capacity, capital, and credibility. Those that cannot will fall behind, regardless of ambition.

This book arrives at the exact moment when the industry must mature from expansion to **repeatable delivery**.

What Makes this Book Different

Written by a **renewable energy project executioner with direct delivery accountability**, not a consultant or analyst

Grounded in **real execution experience** across land, grid, EPCs, governance, people, and risk

Supported by project realities

Focused on leadership behavior, culture, and systems—not theory or checklists

It occupies a clear white space between

- Technical manuals and leadership books
- Policy commentary and project management textbooks
- Optimistic narratives and execution reality

Why Publishers Should Care

This book has

- Strong relevance for a fast-growing, capital-intensive sector
- A clearly defined professional audience (CEOs, CXOs, PMs, EPC leaders, investors)
- High potential for **corporate bulk sales**, executive education, and conference ecosystems
- Long shelf life as a **reference book for execution leadership**

Most importantly, it addresses a problem that the industry *knows exists* but has not articulated with clarity or courage.

The Core Message

Technology enables renewable energy.

Policy directs it.

Capital accelerates it.

But **execution—led by disciplined leaders and strong culture—decides who succeeds.**

This book matters because it tells that truth clearly, practically, and at the moment the industry most needs to hear it.

Why the Industry Needs this Conversation—Now

The renewable energy sector has reached an inflection point.

For the first time, scale is no longer the primary challenge.

Discipline is.

During the last decade, speed mattered more than structure.

Capacity additions mattered more than delivery systems.

Announcements mattered more than execution readiness.

That era is ending.

The coming phase will expose which organizations built execution capability—and which simply built portfolios.

This book matters because it forces the industry to confront that transition honestly.

The Hidden Risk to India's Renewable Ambition

India's renewable ambition is not fragile because of technology or policy.

It is fragile because of organizational maturity.

Gigawatts can be awarded in tenders.

But gigawatts cannot be delivered through

- Optimistic schedules
- Fragmented ownership
- Informal escalation
- Habitual firefighting
- Dependency on individual heroes

The true risk to national energy targets is not project viability.

It is delivery reliability.

This book reframes that risk in language leaders recognize: execution design.

Why Execution is the New Strategy

In a compressed-tariff world, strategy can no longer rely on

- Superior equipment selection,
- Slightly better financing terms, or

- Early market entry.

Those advantages erode quickly.

What does not erode quickly is the ability to execute under pressure.

Execution reliability is becoming the real strategy.

This book matters because it explicitly positions execution systems, leadership behavior and organizational culture as strategic assets—not operational hygiene.

The Leadership Gap this Book Addresses

Most leadership programs in the energy sector still focus on

- Vision,
- Stakeholder management,
- And high-level governance.

Very few prepare leaders for

- Uncertain land access,
- Multi-agency evacuation coordination,
- Contractor defensiveness,
- Community resistance,
- Decision paralysis,
- And execution fatigue.

This book addresses that leadership gap directly.

It speaks to the daily reality of leaders who must deliver physical infrastructure—not abstract strategy.

A New Professional Language for Execution

One of the most important contributions of this book is vocabulary.

Readiness.

Interface risk.

Decision latency.

Execution ownership.

Time leakage.

Social license.

Institutional memory.

These are not theoretical concepts.

They are operational lenses.

The renewable sector has long lacked a shared language for execution failure.

Without language, problems remain personal.

With language, they become structural.

This book matters because it gives the industry words for what it already experiences—but struggles to articulate.

Why this Book Matters to CEOs and Boards

For CEOs and boards, execution risk is often invisible until it becomes public.

By the time a project misses commissioning

- Capital has already been deployed,
- Relationships are already strained,
- And credibility is already damaged.

This book provides a way to move execution risk upstream—into leadership conversations, approval processes and governance design.

It helps leaders ask better questions before problems materialize.

Why this Book Matters to Project and Execution Leaders

For project managers and execution leaders, this book validates something many quietly feel:

That most execution failure is not technical incompetence.

It is structural weakness.

This book equips them with

- Language to escalate constructively,
- Frameworks to protect readiness,
- And leadership legitimacy to challenge unsafe speed.

It tells them that execution leadership is not a junior function.

It is the front line of the energy transition.

Why this Book Matters to EPCs, Utilities and Partners

Execution failure rarely belongs to one party.

It is a system failure.

Developers, EPCs, utilities, contractors and authorities all operate inside the same execution environment.

This book invites every participant to see how their behavior contributes to or erodes delivery reliability.

It moves the conversation away from blame and toward system design.

That shift is essential if the sector is to mature collaboratively.

Why this Book Matters to Investors and Lenders

Investors and lenders increasingly recognize that financial risk in renewable energy is deeply tied to execution risk.

Delays destroy cash flows.

Claims destroy margins.

Social conflict destroys predictability.

Governance failure destroys confidence.

This book helps financial stakeholders understand what execution maturity actually looks like—beyond legal structures and contractual frameworks.

It provides a practical lens to evaluate delivery organizations, not just projects.

Why this Book is Not another Project Management Book

This is not a book about tools.

It is not a book about schedules.

It is not a book about templates.

It is a book about how human systems behave under infrastructure pressure.

Most project management literature assumes stable environments.

Renewable energy execution operates in unstable ones.

This book addresses that reality directly.

Why this Book is Not a Critique of the Sector

This book does not criticize the renewable industry.

It respects it.

It takes the sector seriously enough to challenge it.

The past decade was about proving renewable energy could scale.

The next decade will be about proving it can be delivered reliably, repeatedly and responsibly.

This book is written for that next decade.

The Most Important Shift this Book Seeks to Create

The central shift this book calls for is simple:

From heroics to systems.

From

"We fixed it somehow."

To

"We designed it so it would not fail."

From

"Let us manage it."

To

"Let us design it properly."

From

"We will push harder."

To

"We will prepare better."

This is the maturity transition every infrastructure sector must eventually make.

Renewable energy is now at that point.

Why this Book Will Continue to Matter

Technologies will evolve.

Policy frameworks will change.

Market structures will shift.

But execution complexity will only increase.

Hybrid projects.

Storage integration.

Shared infrastructure.

Stricter grid codes.

Higher community scrutiny.

Deeper financial discipline.

The challenges this book addresses are not temporary.

They are structural.

That is why this book has long relevance beyond current policy cycles.

A Personal Closing Note from the Author's Perspective

This book was not written to demonstrate expertise.

It was written to prevent repetition.

Every chapter exists because the same execution failures continue to surface across different companies, regions and technologies.

The industry already has enough ambition.

What it needs now is discipline.

What it needs is memory.

What it needs is leadership maturity.

This book matters because it speaks to that need directly.

The Final Reason this Book Matters

Because the renewable energy transition is no longer a technical experiment.

It is a national and global infrastructure commitment.

And infrastructure success is never decided by vision alone.

It is decided by how organizations behave when

- Plans break,
- Pressure rises,
- Stakeholders resist,
- And time runs out.

This book matters because it prepares leaders for those moments.

Not with motivation.

With execution truth.

Closing Thought

Renewable energy will define the future.

But execution will define whether that future is built with credibility, confidence and trust.

This book exists to help the industry cross that final—and most difficult—gap.

End of Book